INFORMOTION
ANIMATED
INFOGRAPHICS

EDITED BY
TIM FINKE AND SEBASTIAN MANGER

CO-EDITED BY
STEFAN FICHTEL

gestalten

CONTENT

/EXPLANATION

BLACK MARGINAL NOTES
< cross references within this book

BLUE MARGINAL NOTES
< sources

online content available
(please find a unique code
at the end of this book)

CONTENT

CONTENT

PREFACE by Stefan Fichtel

WELL-MADE ANIMATED INFORMATION GRAPHICS ARE BASED ON CLEAR DECISIONS ABOUT WHAT MATTERS AND WHAT SHOULD BE LEFT OUT.

It is now more than 20 years ago that a 16-year-old student sat captivated in front of his video recorder and kept rewinding a sequence on magnetic tape in order to view it more closely in slow motion. This scene from an information graphic on British television, which probably ended up on a German program more or less by chance and presumably led to a warning to the program director, since it was the trashiest, yet most fascinating series that ever appeared on television in Germany. The scene in question was the explanation of the most powerful animal in the history of the universe, the most destructive creature of all worlds: the Babel fish from *Hitchhiker's Guide to the Galaxy!* > FIG. 1

All this was long before you could make a serious living as an information graphic artist; indeed long before people in Germany had any idea what information graphics could be. The most modern personal computer at the time was the legendary Amiga 500 or the concrete-gray PowerPCs. These were machines with which one could happily waste hours and days without doing anything productive and that tended to complicate workflows instead of simplifying them. Back then information graphics were still produced entirely by hand. That is particularly true of the animations of the Babel fish, which were not digital, but created using the traditional stop-motion technique. ROD LORD, who made these graphics, quite aptly described the milestones of his era's animations: "None of us really knew what computer graphics look like because there weren't any." Yet his animations, including the Babel fish, were the greatest animated information graphics one could imagine at the time.

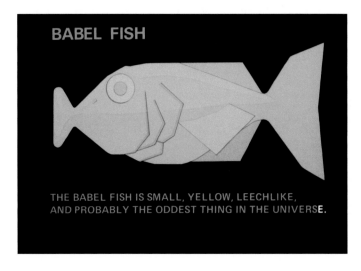

FIG. 1
The most dangerous animal in the history of the universe.

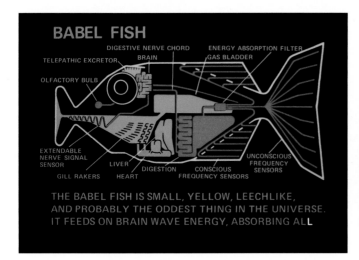

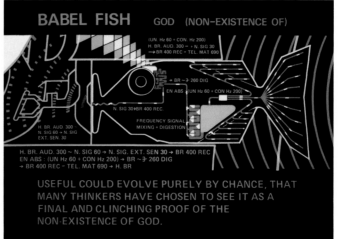

BABEL FISH

DIGESTIVE NERVE CHORD — ENERGY ABSORPTION FILTER
BRAIN
TELEPATHIC EXCRETOR — GAS BLADDER

OLFACTORY BULB

EXTENDABLE
NERVE SIGNAL
SENSOR
LIVER   DIGESTION   CONSCIOUS   UNCONSCIOUS
GILL RAKERS   HEART   FREQUENCY SENSORS   FREQUENCY
                                           SENSORS

THE BABEL FISH IS SMALL, YELLOW, LEECHLIKE,
AND PROBABLY THE ODDEST THING IN THE UNIVERSE.
IT FEEDS ON BRAIN WAVE ENERGY, ABSORBING ALL

BABEL FISH   GOD (NON-EXISTENCE OF)

USEFUL COULD EVOLVE PURELY BY CHANCE, THAT
MANY THINKERS HAVE CHOSEN TO SEE IT AS A
FINAL AND CLINCHING PROOF OF THE
NON-EXISTENCE OF GOD.

FIG. 1

The best proof of their power is that these graphics have lost little of their visionary impact even today. ROD LORD explains why in the same interview:

"It's funny now but I still get asked today to use some of the kind of look and feel from *Hitchhiker's*. [...] Computer graphics today seem to spend an awful lot of energy trying to be as real as possible. Whereas actually, the strength in images is very often in simplicity and in reducing things to the basic requirements rather than trying to dress up it too much."

This encounter with the Babel fish was my first contact with animated information graphics and after I had torn myself away from the video recorder, I soon began to study illustration. But my fascination with information graphics had clearly cooled in the meantime. For me they had shrunk down to stupid bar, pie, and other two-dimensional charts – the very opposite of fun, entertainment, and pleasure in narrative. After finishing my degree – I had since sworn I would never end up as an information graphic artist – it took almost exactly three infinitely long months earning nothing as a freelance illustrator before – from one day to the next – I grabbed the first and best job I could. I had mutated into an information graphic artist overnight and I have never had any doubts about my job since.

Despite all my prejudices, it became clear to me how fascinating information graphics can be; how difficult but exciting it is to discover the stories that are hidden behind numbers and data that shape our lives. While, an Excel spreadsheet still does not exactly have the same attraction for me at first glance that Douglas Adams's sci-fi series once did. But if you manage to make the stories concealed within comprehensible in images, then they have an unsuspected attraction and can captivate many viewers.

Winning people over to a subject matter that had until then meant absolutely nothing to them or seemed far too complicated has remained my constant activity ever since. How does a financial crash occur? How can airplanes that weigh many tons still fly? How much is a billion dollars? Questions we could only answer with difficulty and numbers too vast for us to imagine can be answered intelligibly in explanatory information graphics where clear comparisons can be made. One example of how successful such an explanation can be is PADDY HIRSCH's video on CDOs. > FIG. 2 Any noneconomist will understand within six minutes what triggered the financial crisis of 2008 and how collateralized debt obligations – a phrase we Germans can barely pronounce – could actually work.

A lot of time has passed since ROD LORD's animated stop-motion graphics. Advanced technologies have simplified the work process of packing information into animated graphics, enabling thousands of creative people to tell entertaining, informative stories using cinematic means. At the moment there is a wave of such animated explanatory videos moving through the ether in various media channels. The videos are produced by creative individuals or small teams in schools and professional agencies with the intention of explaining a difficult subject matter, or at least making this specific visual language more interesting.

FIG. 2

More and more companies are using this method to explain to their employees why production processes suddenly have to be changed and what it means for individuals. Advertising agencies are developing trailers about how abstract products can be helpful. In order to clarify the functionality and usage of overcomplicated products advertising agencies embrace infographics rather than photo or video imagery of the actual product. Hollywood films such as *Stranger than Fiction* or *Ironman*, commercials by Areva, Adidas, or Siemens, and even music videos, by Röyksopp, for example, all make use of the specific aesthetic of animated information graphics in order to create a look that is preferably informative and of contemporary relevance. After 20 years, entertainment value has finally become part of the art of the information graphic. Moreover, current findings in brain research demonstrate that communicating via several channels of perception can significantly improve the absorption of information. Information graphics present part of the content on a visual level, which the brain can decode faster and store better than it can with abstract text or unclear photographs alone.

This all sounds almost too perfect, but on the path to more efficient communication, we are often miles away from the potential. Due to enhanced technological conditions pretty much every informtion graphic can be realized today. However, in regards to form and content, the process of visualizing information remains difficult and often problematic. It is not just about having an illustration that is as spectacular as possible, but also about presenting the content in a catchy and clear way. There seems to be a considerable lack of knowledge about how to achieve this. Often, designers lack not only knowledge about what the target audience is capable of absorbing but also the most basic knowledge of how data is visualized in the first place. Aspects that do not fit are made to fit rather than suited with an appropriate form that really communicates their content. Elements that look boring are quickly clothed in a magnificent glitter dress, with a result that hides information behind pretty pictures, hinders the viewers comprehension and thus fails to meet the basic requirements of the informative narrative. There is no hint whatsoever of how good it could have been, and, as noted above, the subject matter is quickly forgotten.

This often leaves open the very questions that were supposed to be clarified: Where is the data from and who selects it? What is the story? What is the core message and what is the producer trying to achieve? How do I create a viable plot? Who writes the text and is it read in a way that suits my animation? Are my comparisons appropriate and comprehensible enough to be grasped immediately? The exciting field of animated information graphics thus calls not only just for the abilities of a graphic designer, but also for those of a director and a journalist.

But this book is not another attempt to explain how to develop an information graphic properly. Although there is no one comprehensive standard work on the subject, there are now sufficient sources providing the necessary basic knowledge. We are trying to show the diversity of possible visualizations in animated explanatory films and which aspects should be considered when communicating specific information in a moving image. To this date there has been no guide of what is possible in a moving image and how it can be done properly. To fill that gap the authors have brought together information about the design and reception of graphics and films, as well as exemplary scenes from all over the world.

Not all works presented in this book should be considered prime examples of their field. While some are successful in every respect, others have been chosen in view to very particular, well executed aspects such as specific visualizations or narrative techniques. > FIG. 3 All the films in this book share a visionary spirit and an impulse for narrative and design. As particularly strong examples in their specefic fields, they are meant to inspire our readers and expand their idea of what information graphics can look like. This book's contribution will be to explain the factors that must be considered to ensure that good aesthetics result in a good educational animation. Only those who make decisions consciously will avoid becoming a victim of chance and arbitrariness. Well-made, animated information graphics are based on clear decisions about what matters and what needs to be left out as unnecessary and therefore detrimental information.

FIG. 3
A good understanding of the basic rules of infographic design is fundamental to the development of efficient animated infographics.

COMMON MISTAKES OF VISUAL REPRESENTATION

Correct values represented by false visual relations.

Correct visual relations with adjusted, but factually false values.

Correct representation of values and their visual relations.

Why?

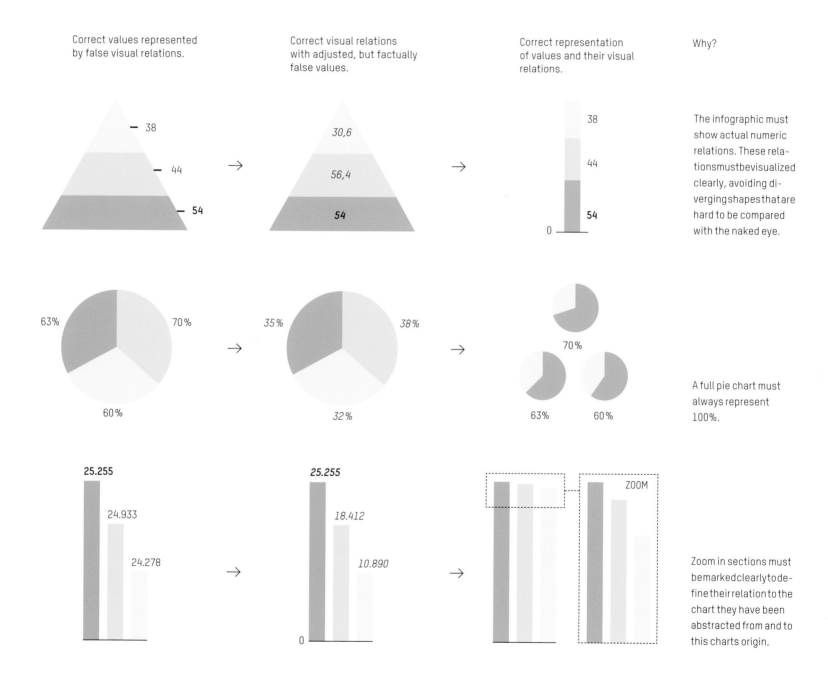

The infographic must show actual numeric relations. These relations must be visualized clearly, avoiding diverging shapes that are hard to be compared with the naked eye.

A full pie chart must always represent 100%.

Zoom in sections must be marked clearly to define their relation to the chart they have been abstracted from and to this charts origin.

A/

/CONTENT

INTRODUCTION

468 CHARACTERS

HOW TO BUILD A PAPER AIRPLANE

1-3

Fold the paper in half lengthwise and run thumbnail along the fold to crease it sharply. Then, unfold the paper.

4-6

Fold the two edges toward the center line. Then, fold the plane in half again.

7-8

Create a wing crease that begins at the nose as shown. Form 3-dimensional shape as shown in figure and the paper airplane is complete. Add finishing touches to your liking or bend up the tailing edge of the wings for lift if your plane has a tendency to nose-dive.

1 INFOGRAPHIC

HOW TO BUILD A PAPER AIRPLANE

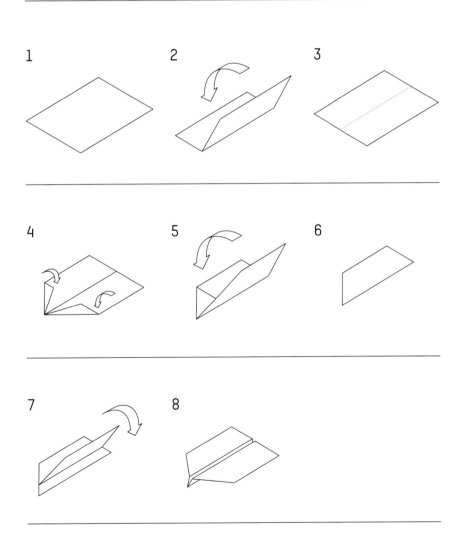

A1 /
INFOGRAPHIC
A PICTURE IS WORTH A THOUSAND WORDS.

This famous saying is often cited to explain the terms *information graphic* and *infographics*. The example on the previous spread illustrates this idea. The complex verbal description of a process as simple as constructing a paper airplane can only be understood if the reader already has some experience folding paper airplanes. The series of images next to it, a step-by-step explanation in pictures, will guide someone with no experience whatsoever to the goal.

The information graphic begins to be effective when the text – either alone or in combination with photographs – does not easily and understandably describe a situation. For example, oral directions can lead to many misunderstanding whereas a map of a city provides a quick and unmistakable overview that is relatively easy to absorb and memorize. Travelers from many countries can use this information without linguistic barriers. This demonstrates the strength of an information graphic. Humans process visual data quicker and more naturally than abstract textual information which is why information graphics feel so straightforward and comprehensible to us. It shortens the path to understanding and in many cases makes it possible in the first place.

liftoff

Newspaper journalism in particular has been exploiting this advantage for a long time. A graphic published in the *Times* of London on the Blight murder case of 1806 is considered one of the first of its kind. It showed a floor plan that clearly illustrated the sequence of events during the murder. This information graphic has since become a standard feature of print and photojournalism. On the one hand, it can convey complex subject matter to a readership with specialized training in a field; on the other hand, it can make a subject more accessible to an audience that is increasingly influenced by television. The market launches of the newspaper *USA Today* in 1982 and the German news magazine *Focus* in 1993 were reactions to this development. In addition to a general shift from the classic principle of text and image to shorter articles with summary introductions, these newspapers use more information graphics.

Information graphics are found in classic print media, such as newspapers, magazines, scientific publications, and textbooks; many other forms of media would be unthinkable without them. The use of moving images has the advantage that information can be better implanted in the brain. Even the use of the classic moving image can now look back on an 80-year history. <

/ B 1
DEVELOPMENTS

Yet even on television, the number of information graphics is constantly increasing. In that context, they are generally called *animated information graphics*. In science magazines they are used to explain why we get sore muscles or how a hybrid car's engine works. Technical progress furthers the use of such visualizations. Once the production of such graphics was subject to more limited computer power; nowadays creating animated weather and election maps or illustrating plays on sports broadcasts based on the most current data, are all a matter of using modern hardware and software.

But a broad spectrum of possibilities is not always synonymous with quality content. For example, it seems that more value is placed on outward appearance than on communicating the subject matter. In the field of animated information graphics, for instance, there are no guidelines to dictate the factors that improve the viewer's absorption of the information.

Just like television, the internet has decisively altered the use of media: information is available all the time and everywhere; it is consumed more quickly on a large number of digital terminals. To keep the viewer's attention these terminals have to be designed accordingly. This opens up a number of possibilities and new challenges. Internet presences such as that of the *New York Times*, for example, have been employing a growing number of interactive information graphics for some time to design content in a way that can be experienced more directly.

This book opens the door to animated information graphics and gives the designer the tools necessary to create them. To that end, it explains not only the most important fundamentals of perception and the general requirements for a moving image but also a number of design possibilities such as the use of animation, voice over, and sound that only a moving medium can offer.

Information design describes a broad field. This book concerns just one subsection: information graphics in passive moving images. In order to define it clearly, it is worthwhile to look at the various ways information can be visualized. The spectrum ranges from the presentation of complex data sets – such as the behavior of an online community of users – by way of a cross section of the detailed structure of a building, to a simple data sets, such as election results or stock prices. The complexity of the information to be processed crucially influences the choice of presentation. To that end, the possibilities for presentation, and their advantages and disadvantages, are explained in the Chapter B1 "Forms of Representation." <

/ B1
FORMS OF
REPRESENTATION

A 1.1 / INFORMATION GRAPHICS

Here one distinguishes between static, interactive, and animated information graphics, the last of which are the subject of the present book.

In contrast to the data visualization discussed in the next section, in which every numerical value has exactly one visual representative, the information graphic presents overall contexts and is often the result of a journalistic examination of a specific thematic area. By comparing different data sets and visualizations of the data and embedding them in a context, the viewer sees the result in the form of a narration with the help of illustrations.

Much like information visualization, there are hardly any automated applications that make it possible to bring together different data, facts, and illustrations. The information graphic also offers more space for illustration and narration. It concentrates on a specific intention to communicate a set of facts whose meaning is supposed to be revealed in as short a span as possible.

A 1.2 / DATA VISUALIZATION

Data visualization makes use of various (representative) tools, ranging from traditional programs, like Illustrator, to internet collaboration tools such as Many Eyes, flare, R-Project, and Prefuse. What they all have in common is that they exclusively prepare complex data sets in a visual way. In addition to classic and more experimental forms, using computer-aided processing of large quantities of data to form complex visualizations has proven to be an especially powerful tool. Programming languages like Processing[1] facilitate the process of data visualization, focussing on structure and on bunching complex data sets.

Such visualizations are well suited to supporting journalistic work, providing the opportunity to make large volumes of data tangible in the first place. Data visualizations are often the basis for an information graphic or part of a more complex one.

---

1   Processing is a specialized object-oriented, highly standardized programming language and an essential element of the integrated developing environment for the areas of graphics, simulation, and animation.

THIS BOOK
FOCUSES ON ANIMATED INFORMATION GRAPHICS THAT HAVE A LINEAR STRUCTURE AND ARE NOT INFLUENCED BY THE USER.

A 1.3 / DEFINITION

This book focuses on animated information graphics that, on the one hand, have a linear structure and, on the other hand, are not influenced by the user. Such graphics are found on television, for example, extending from the science magazine by way of news broadcasts to edutainment formats. In addition, however, animated information graphics are increasingly employed in internet product presentations and in apps for the internet presences of renowned magazines.

In order to convey every bit of information and ensure its perception by the viewer, such information graphics have to work within a fixed time span.

As a result, the premises and requirements are very different from those of the design of interactive information graphics.

The aforementioned definition points to a clearly delimited area of possibilities for communicating the intended message in a passive moving image. Before a designer decides to make an information graphic under these conditions, he or she must be aware of the associated advantages and disadvantages: which design options contribute to a targeted communication of information and which detract from it. Among other things, Chapter B4 "Basic Conditions of the Moving Image" describes the basic conditions for the medium of moving images and provides information on the possibilities and limitations of the passive moving image. <

/ B 4
BASIC CONDITIONS
OF THE MOVING IMAGE

To that end, the following spread provides an overview of the pros and cons of the passive moving image that should be considered when creating an animated information graphic.

PROS

TIME SEQUENCES

Temporal sequences of events can be rendered graphically. In addition, time can be slowed or accelerated at will to emphasize or speed up processes.

CAUSALITY

Relationships and interdependencies of data and processes can be illustrated more directly.

DIRECTING THE VIEWER

Viewers are directed to selected facts in a predetermined sequence, resulting in fewer misunderstandings in interpreting the graphic.

EXPRESSION

The physical makeup of an object or the way it moves can be illustrated with animations.

VARYING TECHNIQUES OF DEPICTION

Techniques used in information graphics, such as cross sections or exploded views, can be combined in a temporal sequence.

CHANGING PERSPECTIVES

Camera angles can be used to observe and explain facts from different perspectives.

LANGUAGE / SOUND

The spoken word establishes a personal connection to the viewers. Language and sound support and emphasize the depiction.

CONS

VIEWING TIME

The viewer has a limited amount of time available to perceive the content. Because everyone perceives at a different rate, some of them may not understand.

LINEARITY

Viewers are only referred to a selection of facts. Because the time frame is fixed, they often cannot learn anymore.

COMPLEXITY

Especially when dealing with statistical data, it is more difficult to convey complexity in a moving image than in static or interactive graphics, since only a certain time frame is available. Sequences that are too long will tire the viewers, since they cannot control the sequence or the amount of information.

MANIPULATION

Vieweres are unable to examine the data or the depicted processes more closely. They lack the opportunity to question what the graphic intends to convey. The time limitation can thus be exploited deliberately to communicate false information.

A2 /
DEVELOPMENTS

INFORMATION GRAPHICS
IS AN OFT-CITED
DESIGN DISCIPLINE.

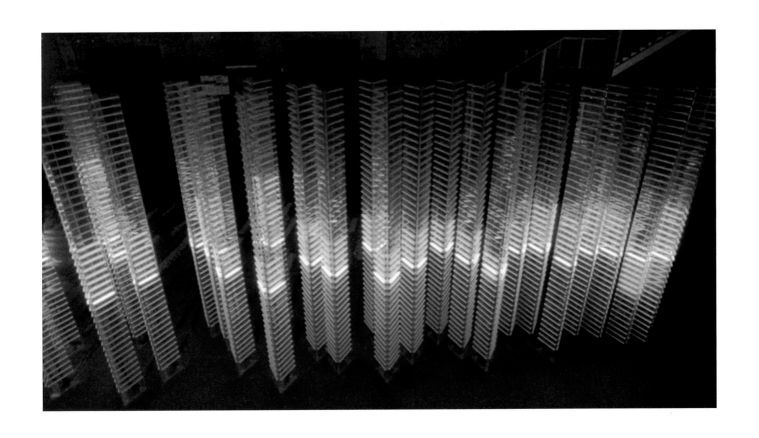

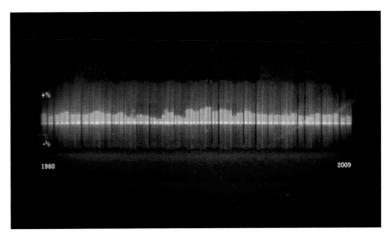

TITLE **DUELITY**

CATEGORY school project

DESIGNER Ryan Uhrich

PRODUCED AT Vancouver Film School

DESCRIPTION According to the records of the General Organization of Development labs (GOD) it took a mere six days to manufacture a fully-operational universe, complete with day, night, flora and fauna, and to install Adam as its manager for overseeing daily functions on Earth. That's one story.

If thou shalt believe the Book of Darwin, it's five billion years after The Big Bang that we behold what the cosmos hath begat: the magma, the terra firma, the creeping beasts, and mankind, whose dolorous and chaotic evolution begat the gift of consciousness.

Duelity is an animation that tells both sides of the story of Earth's origins in a dizzying and provocative journey through the history and language that marks human thought.

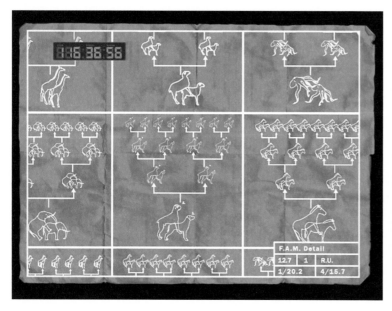

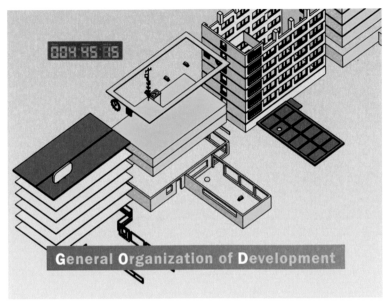

General Organization of Development

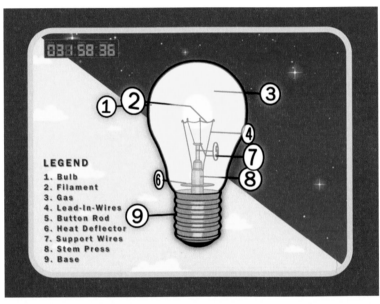

LEGEND
1. Bulb
2. Filament
3. Gas
4. Lead-In-Wires
5. Button Rod
6. Heat Deflector
7. Support Wires
8. Stem Press
9. Base

TITLE **61 SHOTS**

CATEGORY commercial

CLIENT City of Madrid

STUDIO TRESRAZONES

DESCRIPTION Imagine a new language that would make it possible to explain sports with cinematographic narratives to provide a new experience to users in visual information.

THE SHOT. The idea is to translate the main keys needed to understand a sport discipline into a short clip. In no more than a minute, in order to maintain the viewer's attention, we should translate the information in three ways:

1. Voice over that explains the audiovisual info graphic.
2. Visual data that supports concepts, e.g. numerals, charts, and evolutions.
3. Main athletic animation that uses slow motion, different perspectives, and details.

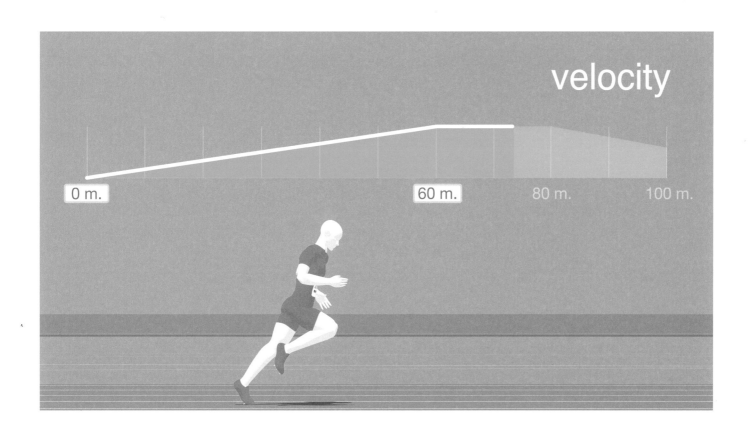

velocity

0 m.   60 m.   80 m.   100 m.

35

TITLE
MATTA –
RELEASE THE FREQ

CATEGORY   music video

DESIGN   Kim Holm

DESCRIPTION   This video is based on the idea of humanizing deer, using their pure majestic expression accompanied by human perceptions of nature in the form of infographics and statistics.

Kim Holm demonstrates how humans make use of and benefit from animals by putting them into systems foreign to their species. All this with a slightly humoristic undertone, to make a point of this not being a political message, but more like a philosophical study.

This is all intended to work in context with Matta's hard-hitting, dark, and chaotic musical atmosphere.

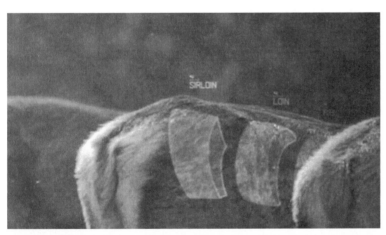

TITLE **OVERFISHING**

CATEGORY infotainment

DESIGN Uli Henrik Streckenbach

DESCRIPTION The fish population in the sea has significantly declined. In the case of large fish like tuna and cod, numbers have decreased by 90 percent within 50 years, scientists report. Many species could disappear entirely if fishing is not massively restricted. Yet many people are entirely unaware of this. The film *Die Überfischung der Meere (The overfishing of the seas)* illustrates the alarming facts and statistics of industrial fishing in order to raise more attention on the subject.

In order to reach many people – including those who have not previously been interested in the topic – it was important to present the theme in a way that viewers would become engaged with it.

This animated film was based on studies by Greenpeace, data from the WWF, and research by the British documentary filmmaker Rupert Murray and the American author Jonathan Safran Foer; the voice over was spoken by Hilmar Eichhorn, an actor at the *Neues Theater* in Halle an der Saale. By combining a spoken text with moving images, a great deal of information could be conveyed in a more concise and exciting way.

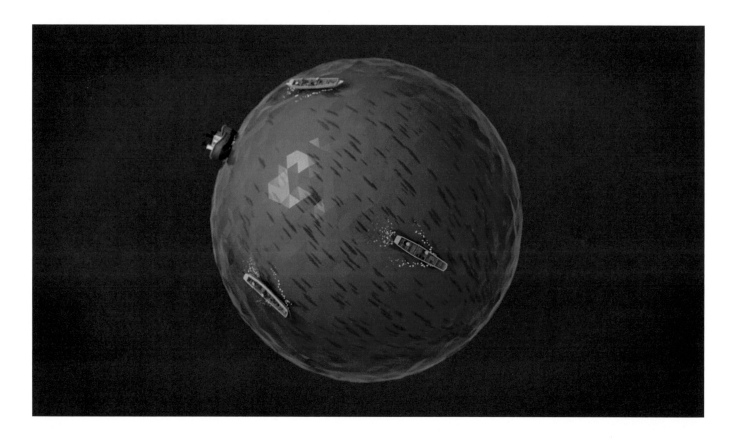

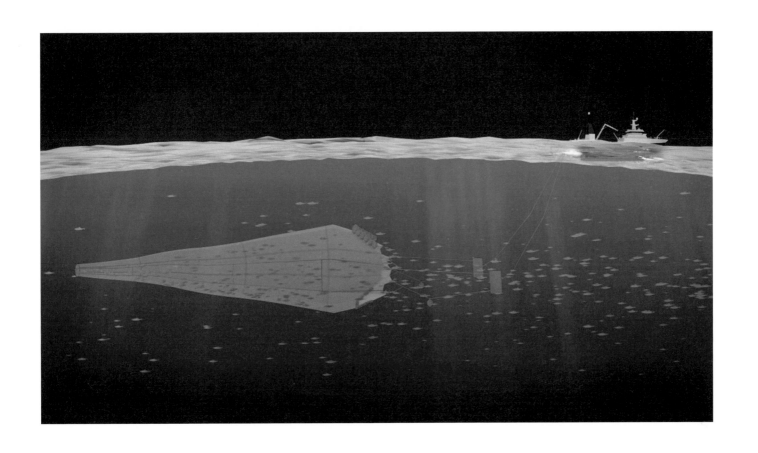

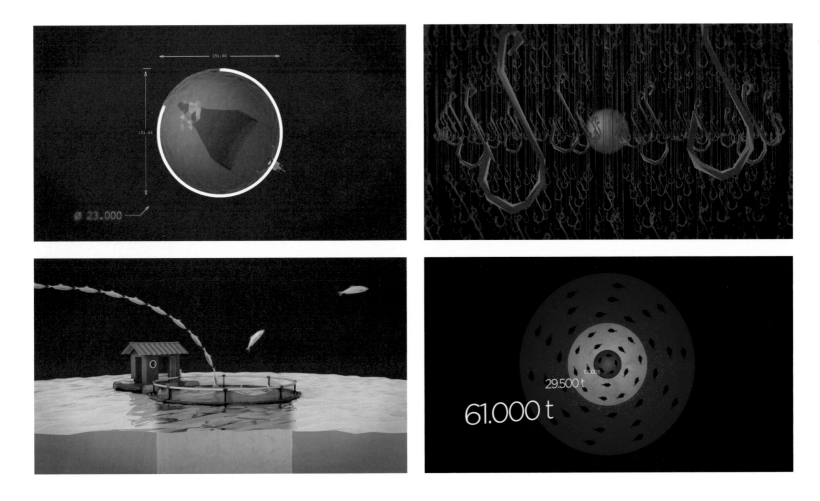

TITLE **F1 2011 RED BULL RACING – MY INNER SECRETS – KERS & REARWING**

CATEGORY   infotainment

CLIENT   Red Bull Media House GmbH – Andi Gall

STUDIO   Peter Clausen Film & TV Produktions-GmbH

DESCRIPTION At the beginning of the 2011 season, Red Bull Racing started the first filmic F1-Racing Encyclopaedia as a series: directly out of the cockpit and in full racing action, Sebastian Vettel and Mark Webber explain enthralling topics such as aerodynamics, tires, and KERS.

The RB7 racing car becomes transparent and reveals his inner secrets with glowing brake pads, hammering pistons, and complex technical actions usually invisible.

OVERTAKING

DISTANCE
00:00:85

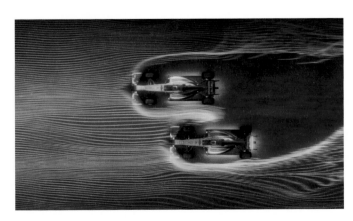

TITLE
THE RED BULL AIR RACE WORLD CHAMPIONSHIP

CATEGORY infotainment

CLIENT Red Bull Media House GmbH – Andi Gall

STUDIO Peter Clausen Film & TV Produktions-GmbH

DESCRIPTION The fastest motorsport in all three dimensions. Gravity-defying racing at breakneck speed only a few meters above the ground.
This computer-animated clip features Air-Race pilot Kirby Chambliss as he races heart-stoppingly through the aerial track. Besides demonstrating how challenging it is to fly these race planes, the animation introduces the Red Bull Air Race's set of rules.

TITLE **WIM•BLE•DON**

CATEGORY infotainment

DESIGN Bryan Ku

DESCRIPTION This is an experimental infographic documenting the final game in the 122nd edition of the Wimbledon Championships Men's Final between tennis giants Rafael Nadal and Roger Federer.

TITLE **IHG – WHAT IS GREEN ENGAGE?**

CATEGORY commercial

CLIENT InterContinental Hotels Group

STUDIO Dachis Group

DESCRIPTION Innovation is key to the strategy of the InterContinental Hotels Group. Dachis Group approach communications in the same way, portraying leadership through innovation. A series of animated videos, created in collaboration with the visual thinking agency XPLANE, was chosen as an engaging platform to help achieve the communication objectives. Through animation and information design Dachis Group were able to develop a specific look and feel and to use as few words as possible. The resulting consistent visual language engages a variety of stakeholders.

IMAGINE HOTELS THAT
LISTEN TO THE COMMUNITY...

TITLE
CANAL ISABEL II – THE WATER CYCLE

CATEGORY infotainment

CLIENT Canal Isabel II

STUDIO binalogue

DESCRIPTION Canal Isabel II, the company in charge of Madrid's water supply, commissioned Binalogue with the animation concept, compositioning, and finishing of this infographics piece, with the art direction and design as well as the development of both 3-D and motion graphics.

The piece is part of a six-minute video developed by different studios. Binalogue's part explains the processing cycle water goes through in La Comunidad de Madrid, from its collection to its purification.

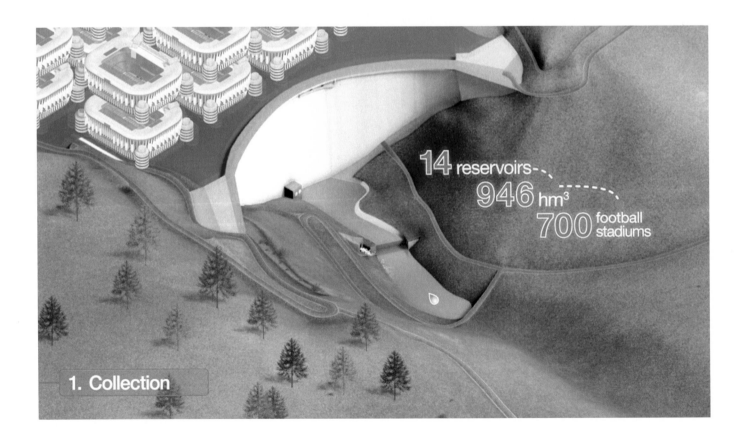

14 reservoirs
946 hm³
700 football stadiums

1. Collection

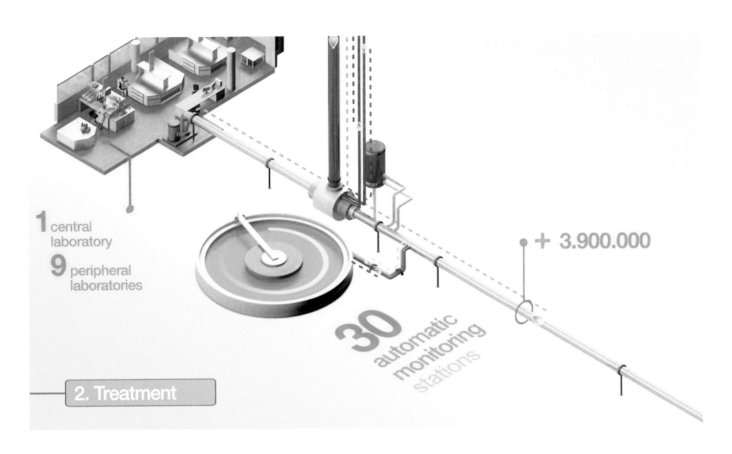

1 central laboratory

9 peripheral laboratories

+ 3.900.000

30 automatic monitoring stations

2. Treatment

530 km of canals & large pipes

+15.000 km network distribution

it would stretch to Australia if placed end to end

20 lifting stations

22

3.

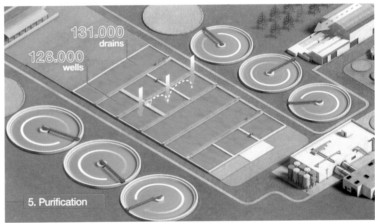

131.000 drains

128.000 wells

5. Purification

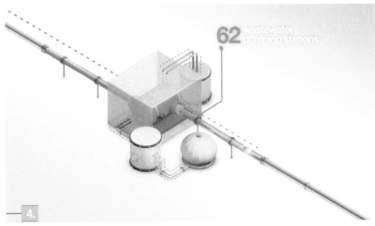

62 wastewater pumping stations

4.

TITLE **CENTRO DE LA TIERRA**

CATEGORY infotainment

CLIENT Discovery Channel Latinamerica / U.S. Hispanics

STUDIO NoBlink

DESCRIPTION This piece was created for Experiencia Discovery, a Discovery Channel online program that experiments with new ways of storytelling, using each and every new media format available. Research and scripting were key components for this topic, which could only be approached as a hypothetical fiction based on factual data, since mankind still has not reached the center of the planet. Something similar to what 1960s movies did with flying cars towards the year 2000.

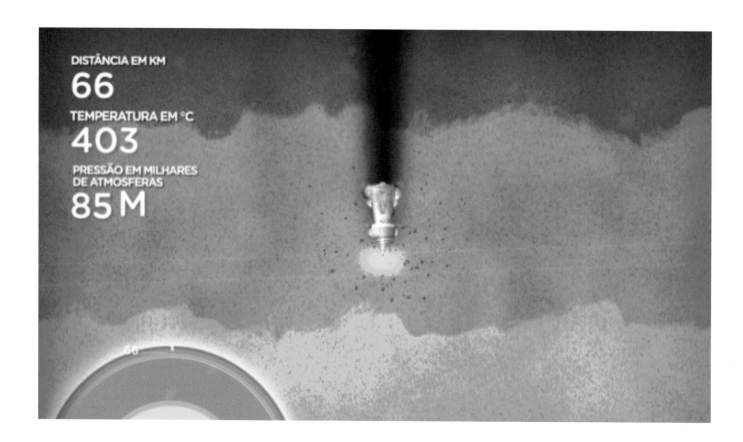

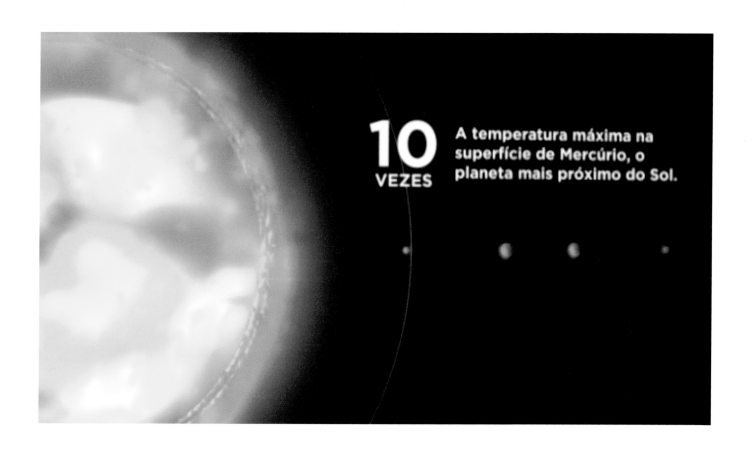

10 VEZES A temperatura máxima na superfície de Mercúrio, o planeta mais próximo do Sol.

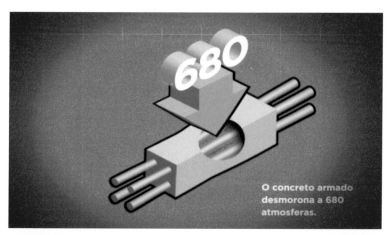

680 O concreto armado **desmorona** a 680 atmosferas.

DISTÂNCIA EM KM
1437

TEMPERATURA EM °C
2425

PRESSÃO EM MILHARES DE ATMOSFERAS
722 M

1437

TRAJE DE FYREPEL
Resiste até 1.100 °C. Ele permitiria quase chegar à parte mais externa do manto superior.

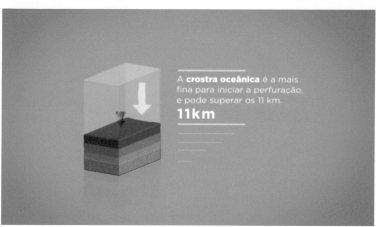

A **crostra oceânica** é a mais fina para iniciar a perfuração, e pode superar os 11 km.
11km

TITLE

FAITES LE BON GESTE ÉCOLOGIQUE

CATEGORY   infotainment

CLIENT   Ecologic

STUDIO   H5

DESCRIPTION   H5 recently finished a corporate movie for an eco-organization dedicated to the recovery, the recycling and the valorization of DEEE (waste of electrics and electronics equipment). This includes schematic diagrams and charts, all illustrated in simple 2-D and isometric visual style, telling the story of a computer's life at a treatment factory, and showing how electrical object are recycled. This film is an evolution of H5's already known clips Areva and Röyksopp. But unlike those two films, the aim was to make a film based on restrictions: H5 worked without Ligne claire, in a restrained color range, and used the CGI (Computer-Generated Imagery) as little as possible.

The overall feel is that of an aesthetic film, every frame of which could be printed. What's great about such a visual language is the variety of possible graphic interpretations.

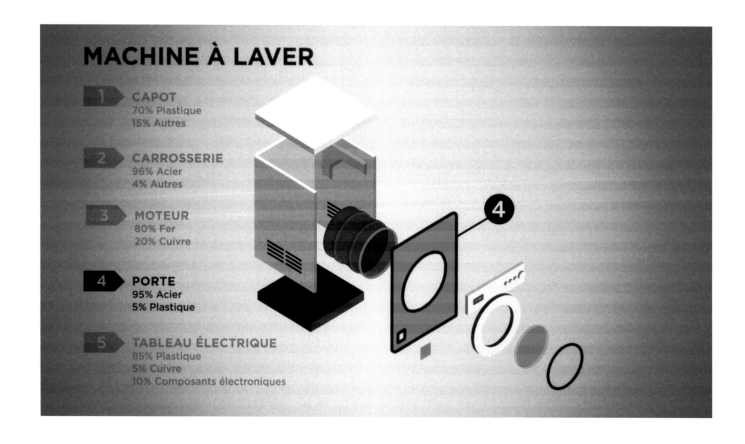

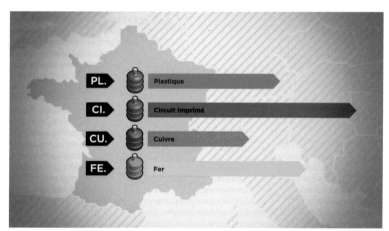

PL. Plastique

CI. Circuit Imprimé

CU. Cuivre

FE. Fer

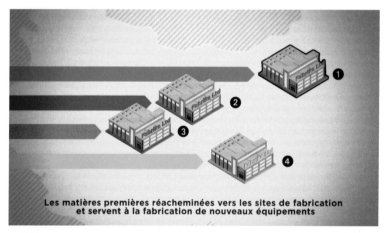

Les matières premières réacheminées vers les sites de fabrication
et servent à la fabrication de nouveaux équipements

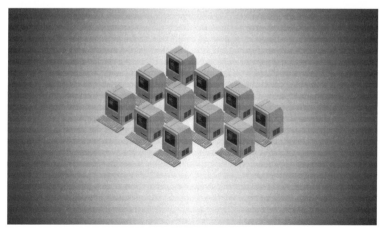

TITLE **BIRDS VS. PLANES**

CATEGORY infotainment

CLIENT Discovery Channel Latin America / U.S. Hispanics

STUDIO NoBlink

DESCRIPTION This piece was created for Experiencia Discovery, a Discovery Channel online program that experiments with new ways of storytelling that use a variety of new media formats. The key concept for this project was to analyze and compare birds and Planes. Both are capable of flying, an ability that has always intrigued mankind.
The amazing information discovered on both sides of the story is shown in the mood of a pre-flight safety video. Which is, by the way, a very interesting example of animated infographics.

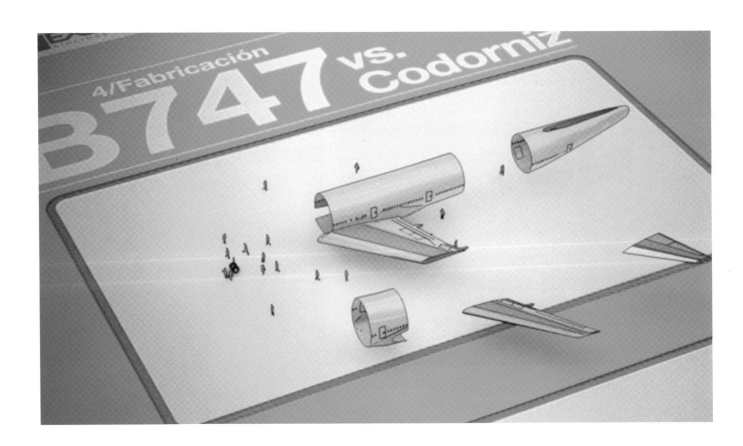

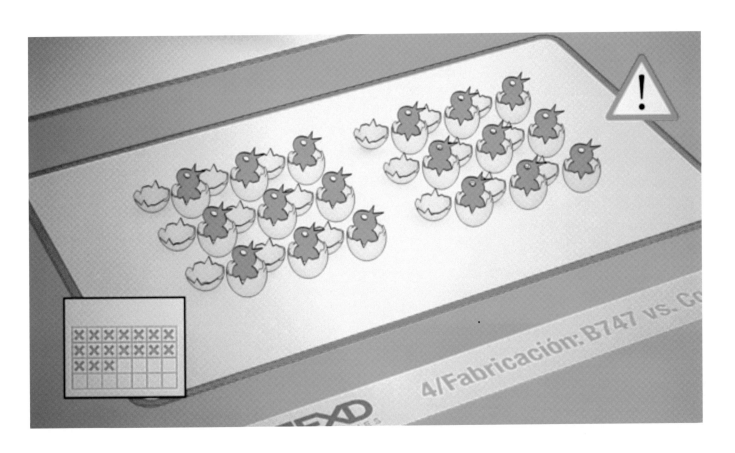

4/Fabricación: B747 vs. Co...

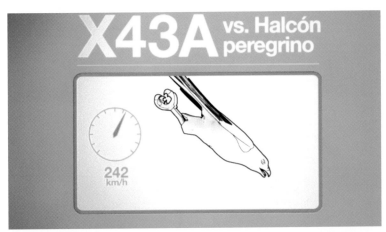

X43A vs. Halcón peregrino

242 km/h

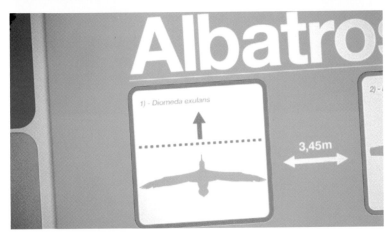

Albatros

1) - Diomeda exulans

3,45m

TITLE **HACK FWD**

CATEGORY infotainment

CLIENT HackFWD

STUDIO IDEO

DESCRIPTION Dreaming about launching a successful startup? Who isn't? And who better to learn from than internet icon Lars Hinrichs. With the help of the design consultancy IDEO, he developed HackFWD, an early-stage investment company specializing in helping the best and most creative developers and coders across Europe to build their own game-changing companies.

To introduce and explain the concept behind HackFWD, this animated graphic takes viewers through the steps and benefits of the process. In doing so, it already follows its own advice: forget about boring presentations.

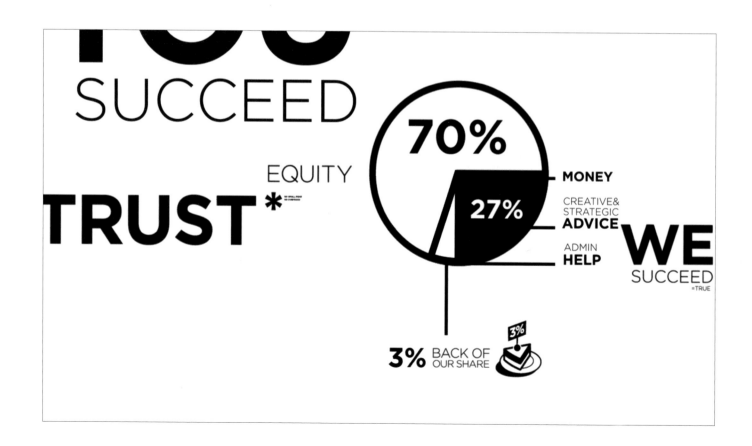

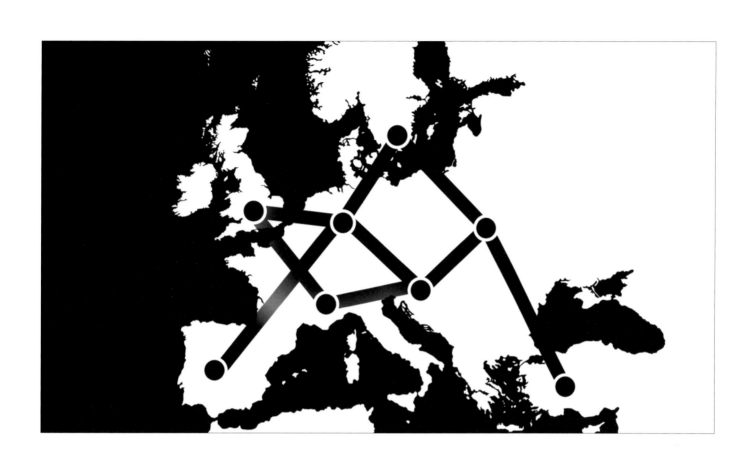

SUCCESSFUL TECH
ENTREPRENEURS

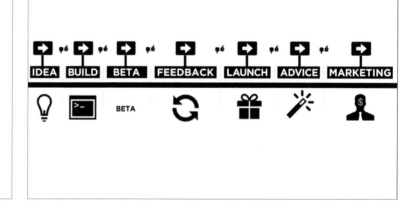

IDEA BUILD BETA FEEDBACK LAUNCH ADVICE MARKETING

BETA

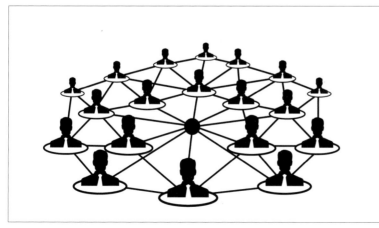

TITLE **STUXNET: ANATOMY OF A COMPUTER VIRUS**

CATEGORY infotainment

CLIENT ABC 1 Australia

STUDIO Patrick Clair

DESCRIPTION This infographic dissects the nature and ramifications of Stuxnet, the first weapon made entirely out of code. This was produced for Australian TV program HungryBeast on Australia's ABC 1.

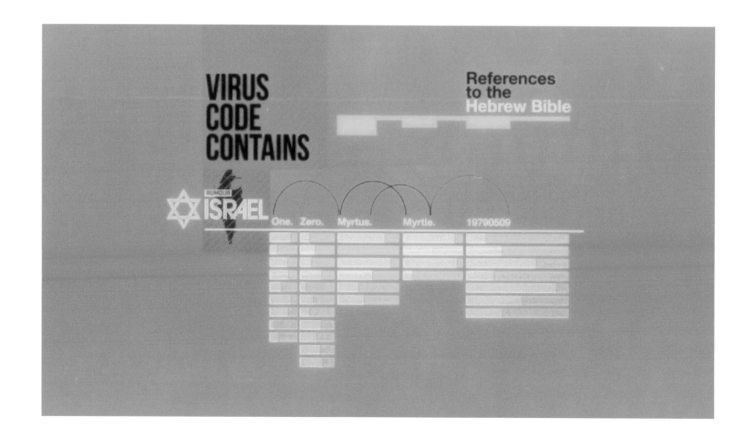

THAT HELP VIRUSES
BURROW INTO SYSTEMS

THE VIRUS MAY HAVE
SHUTDOWN

ISIS INSTITUTE FOR SCIENCE AND
INTERNATIONAL SECURITY

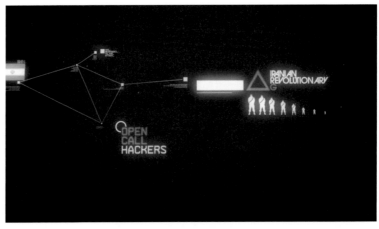

IRANIAN
REVOLUTIONARY

OPEN
CALL
HACKERS

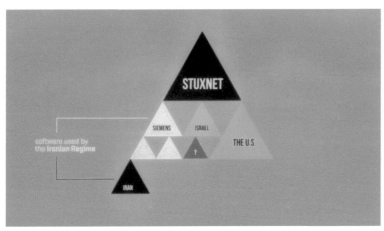

STUXNET

SIEMENS   ISRAEL

software used by
the Iranian Regime   THE U.S

?

IRAN

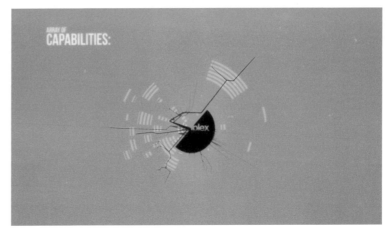

ARRAY OF
CAPABILITIES:

TITLE **LAKS PROJECT**

CATEGORY infotainment

CLIENT Reggio Emilia Municipality

STUDIO TIWI

DESCRIPTION Sponsored by the E.U. within the framework of
the Life Project, this project sets out to help local
municipalities analyze, plan, and improve their cit-
ies' environmental impact on climate change.
A human-friendly scenario helps to understand,
line-by-line each point of this interesting project,
guided by the voice over.

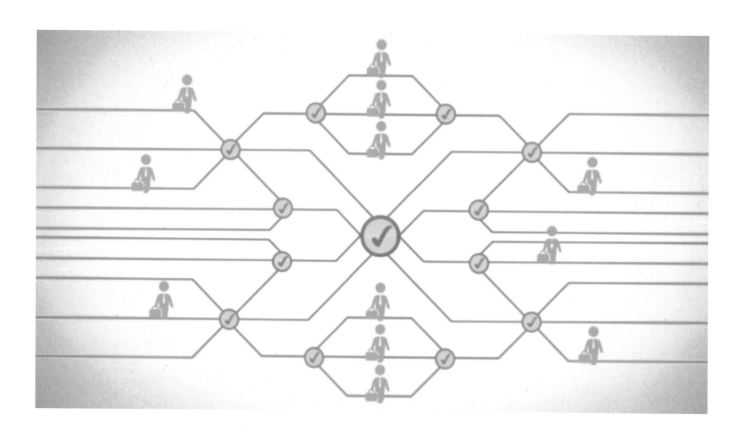

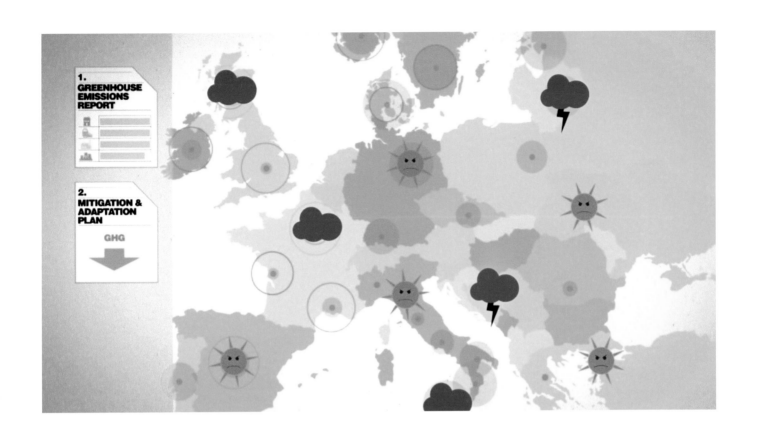

TEC MEETING 2009 –
NEW PORTFOLIO MANAGEMENT

TITLE

CATEGORY — infotainment

CLIENT — T-Systems

STUDIO — KircherBurkhardt

DESCRIPTION — T-Systems has repeatedly undergone extensive changes that have not only affected its product portfolio, but its management, employees, and customers alike. Hence, it is important to communicate this constantly to all the stakeholders in a way they can understand.

Because of the complex product structure, everyone involved in the present films was given a thorough yet succinct overview of the questions: Where do we currently stand? Where do we want to go? How do we achieve that together? Why are we doing it?

These films were first shown at the 2009 TEC-Meeting and mark the beginning of a new, broad communication strategy. The films introduced the audience to the existing workshops and sets of problems. They were then shown to customers at Cebit and later to employees of T-Systems.

The film bears reference to the changes in production that the automobile industry had to cope with roughly 10 years earlier and the great similarities to changes in the ITC sector.

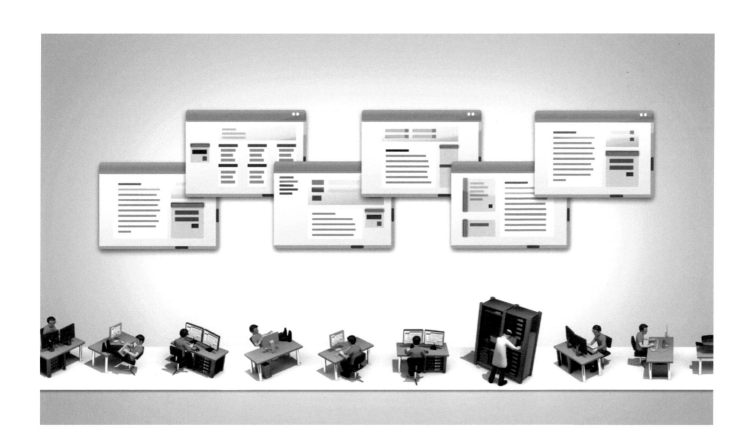

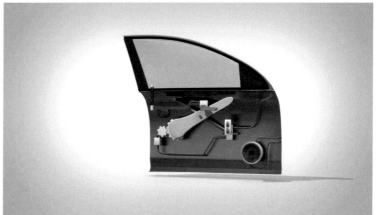

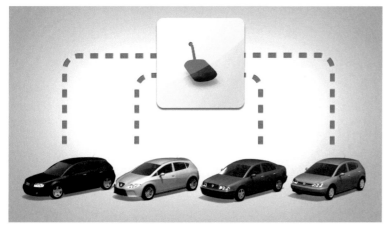

TITLE
SATELLITES: A USERS MANUAL / SECTION 05, WHY WE NEED SATELLITES

CATEGORY
infotainment

CLIENT
Astra

STUDIO
SR/CP Sam Renwick

DESCRIPTION
Based in Luxembourg, Astra is Europe's largest satellite operator. They asked SR/CP Sam Renwick to create a series of films explaining everything about the launching and operation of satellites. SR/CP Sam Renwick's wanted to make films they would have wished to have been shown at school themselves. They focussed on explaining an otherwise extremely complicated process in a very simple, accessible way.

Following their aim of making a potentially mundane and corporate subject interesting, they designed a series of colorful and evocative films based on research and the dry data of technical manuals. Some of their diagrams could be works of art in their own right. For each film the designers and developers of SR/CP Sam Renwick asked theirselves: What would interest us and hold our attention? At script stage they considered different technical executions, but animation appeared to be the most practical, given the diagrammatic content and the fact that much of the narrative takes place 36,000 km above the Earth!

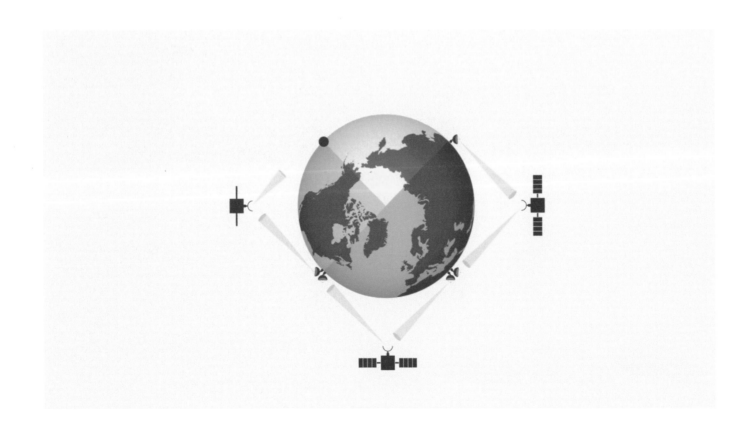

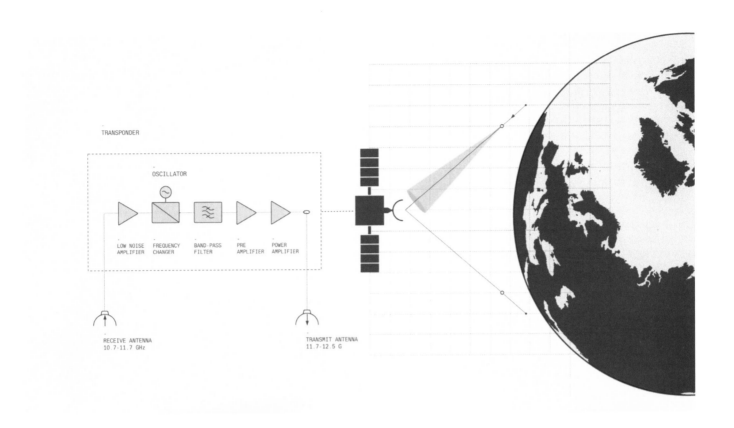

TRANSPONDER

OSCILLATOR

LOW NOISE
AMPLIFIER

FREQUENCY
CHANGER

BAND-PASS
FILTER

PRE
AMPLIFIER

POWER
AMPLIFIER

RECEIVE ANTENNA
10.7-11.7 GHz

TRANSMIT ANTENNA
11.7-12.5 G

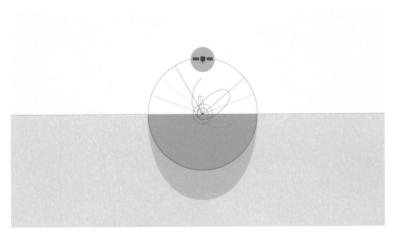

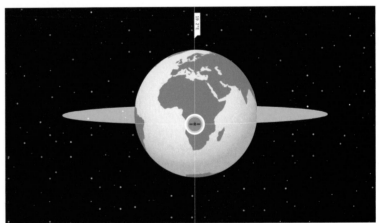

TITLE
HELLMANN'S –
EAT REAL, EAT LOCAL

CATEGORY commercial

CLIENT Hellmann's

STUDIO Crush and Ogilvy & Mather Toronto

DESCRIPTION The multidisciplinary studio Crush has been doing motion graphics for a variety of industries and clients since 1998. Their project for Hellmann's "Eat Real, Eat Local" campaign has been realized in collaboration with Ogilvy & Mather Toronto. The goal was to present startling facts about the food supply chain and to ground the information in an everyday world context—in this case, an "average Canadian dinner table."

The project communicates its content in an exemplary manner, using a variety of forms and a strong narrative structure. The result is a powerful piece of work that changes people's attitudes. The film was very well-received and can be considered an early standard bearer of the Canadian local food movement.

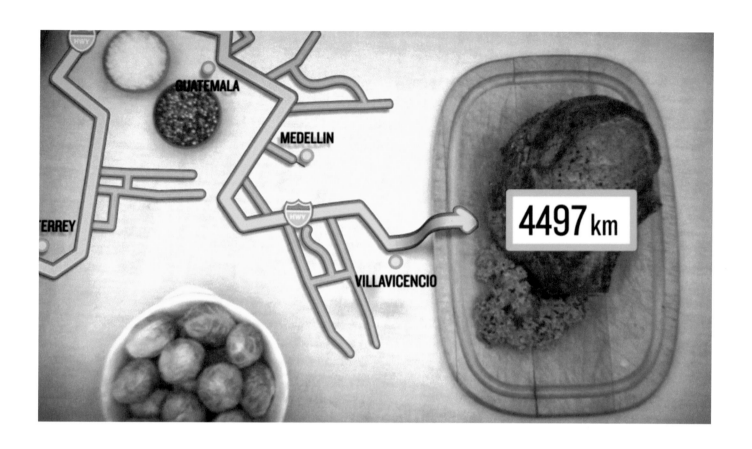

**% OF NET SUPPLY

TITLE
HISTORY OF THE IPHONE

CATEGORY infotainment

CLIENT CNET UK website

STUDIO Headspin Media

DESCRIPTION To coincide with the launch of the iPhone 4S, CBS commissioned Headspin Media to animate a complete history of the iPhone. With regards to animation, Headspin were asked to make use of the increasingly popular infographic style. Using simple animated illustrations alongside detailed text, their infographics give an impression of an animated diagram or instruction manual. The idea with the text is that the important facts are large and easy to read, while the more in-depth information is set in smaller type, giving the viewer the opportunity to pause the video and read. A well-known example of this style of animation is the music video for Röyksopp's "Remind Me." The map introduction in the iPhone infographic is an acknowledgement of this influence.

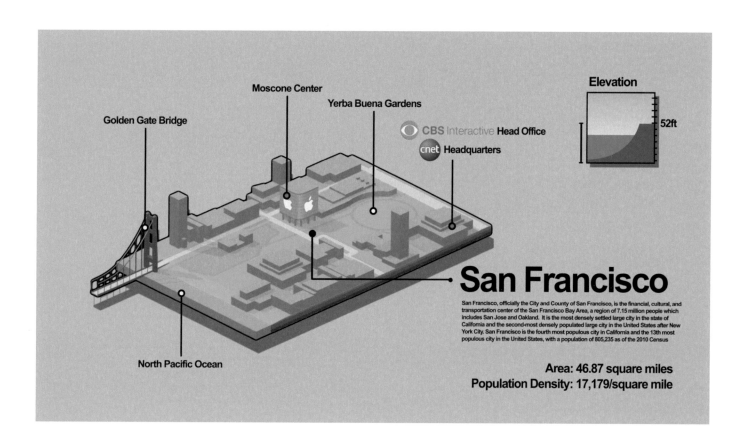

Golden Gate Bridge

Moscone Center

Yerba Buena Gardens

CBS Interactive **Head Office**

cnet **Headquarters**

Elevation

52ft

San Francisco

San Francisco, officially the City and County of San Francisco, is the financial, cultural, and transportation center of the San Francisco Bay Area, a region of 7.15 million people which includes San Jose and Oakland. It is the most densely settled large city in the state of California and the second-most densely populated large city in the United States after New York City. San Francisco is the fourth most populous city in California and the 13th most populous city in the United States, with a population of 805,235 as of the 2010 Census

Area: 46.87 square miles
Population Density: 17,179/square mile

North Pacific Ocean

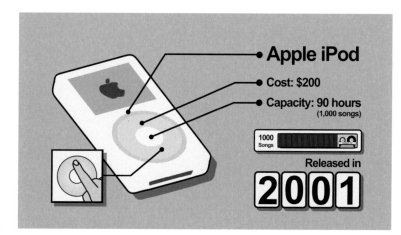

Apple iPod

Cost: $200

Capacity: 90 hours
(1,000 songs)

1000 Songs

Released in

2001

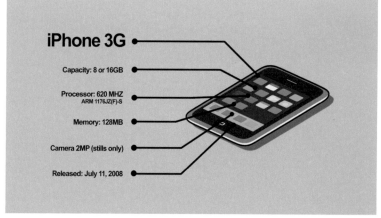

iPhone 3G

Capacity: 8 or 16GB

Processor: 620 MHZ
ARM 1176JZ(F)-S

Memory: 128MB

Camera 2MP (stills only)

Released: July 11, 2008

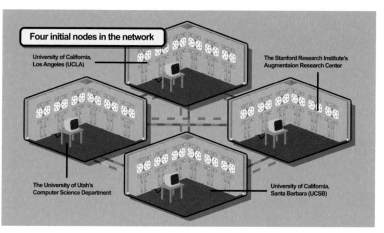

Four initial nodes in the network

University of California,
Los Angeles (UCLA)

The Stanford Research Institute's
Augmentaion Research Center

The University of Utah's
Computer Science Department

University of California,
Santa Barbara (UCSB)

TITLE **TERRAFORM**

CATEGORY school project

DESIGNER Johannes Brückner

PRODUCED AT Hochschule Mannheim

DESCRIPTION The eight-minute-long short film *TerraForm* is concerned with the progress, contradictions, and problems of globalization. The carefully researched facts and complex interconnections are presented in the form of an animated information graphic that is composed of its subjects: people.

The film touches on a sore point of globalized capitalism. On a large scale, globalization can be understood as progress. However, it seems as if only a small part of the population actually benefits from it.

Without offering any preconceived solutions, Johannes Brückner takes his social responsibility as a designer seriously and makes an earnest attempt to stimulate thinking.

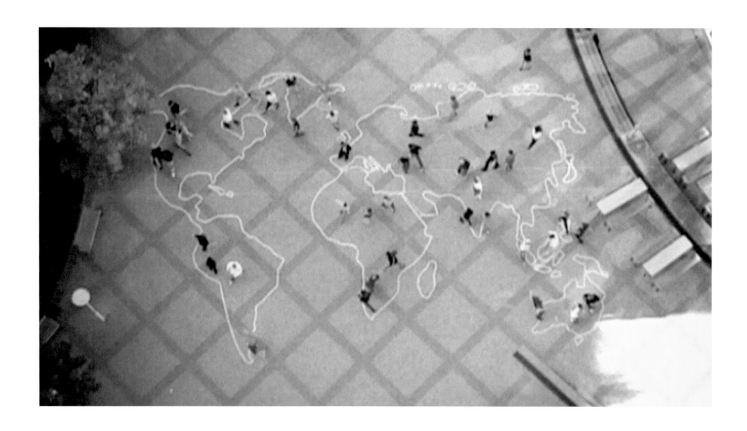

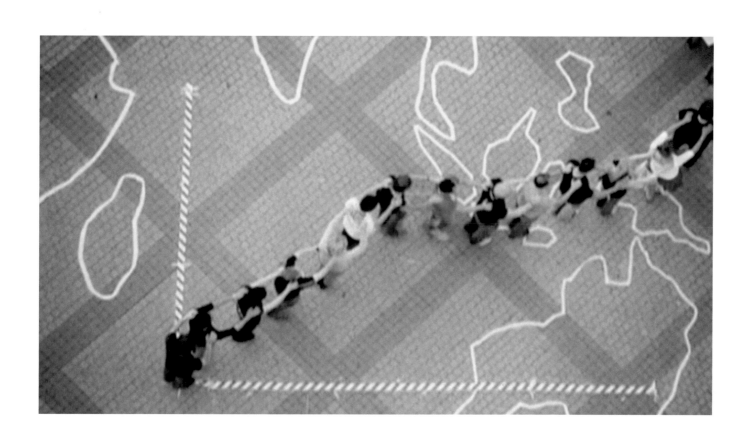

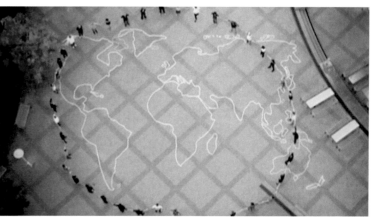

TITLE **UNEXPECTED MUSCULARITY**

CATEGORY science magazine

CLIENT arte TV "X:enius"
AVE Gesellschaft für Fernsehproduktion mbH

STUDIO bitmapboogie

DESCRIPTION Bitmapboogie were in charge of the concept, creative direction, and animation of the motion graphics in this feature story for "X:enius", the popular science magazine on the German/French TV broadcaster arte.
These infographic sequences were part of a documentary with the title *Unexpected Muscularity*. This dealt with how muscles and athletic activity make you faster, more agile, and last but not least happier, activating smart proteins, discharging hormones, and activating certain nerve synapses.

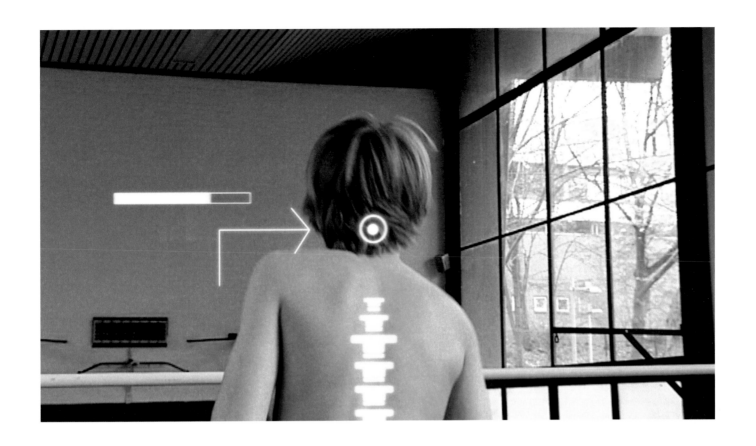

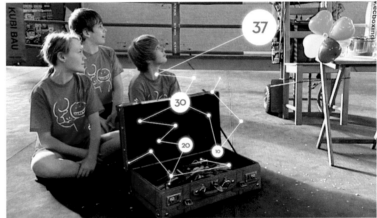

TITLE **CGA CANADA WEST JET**

CATEGORY commercial

CLIENT CGA Canada West Jet

STUDIO crush

DESCRIPTION The project for CGA ist the continuation of a campaign in which real-life certified general accountants' roles in the success of diverse companies are highlighted.
In this case, the company is Westjet, a Canadian airline. The design idea was to incorporate a mixture of financial iconography along with computer graphic miniatures to illustrate areas of the company's business where their accountant was invaluable in achieving its goals.

TITLE
THE CHASER'S "YES WE CANBERRA!"

CATEGORY   opening title

CLIENT   Polar Productions and the Australian Broadcasting Corporation

STUDIO   Patrick Clair, Mick Watson

DESCRIPTION   The animation of *The Chaser's "Yes We Canberra!"* was featured in the opening titles for a political satire television series, screened in the run-up to Australia's national election in 2010. It often seems that Australian politicians are obsessed with polling data and popularity contests. The team recreated a geographically accurate model of Australia's capital city, Canberra, out of nothing but 3-D polling data. The show's title was a pun, so the colors, logo, and feel were inspired by Obama's "Yes We Can" campaign. They use the shared red, white, and blue of the American and Australian flags.

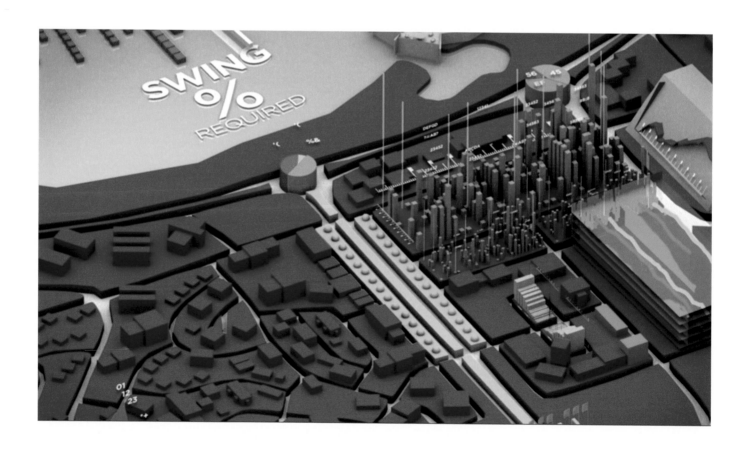

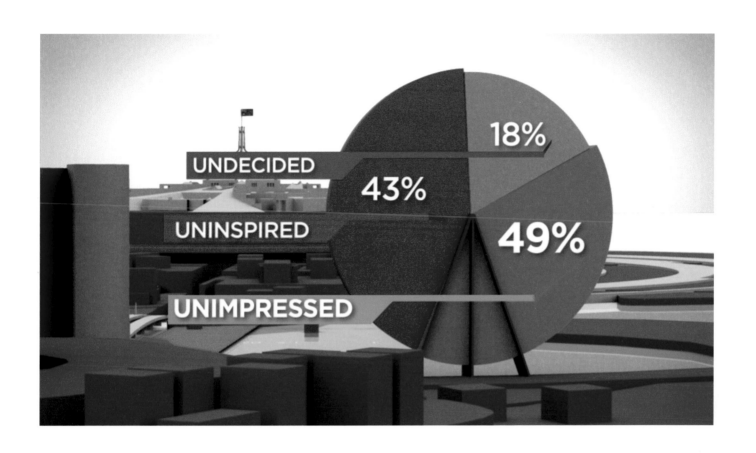

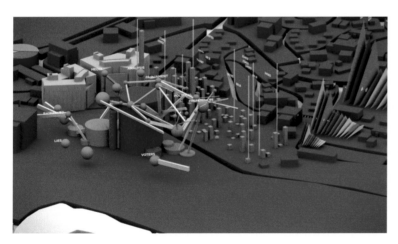

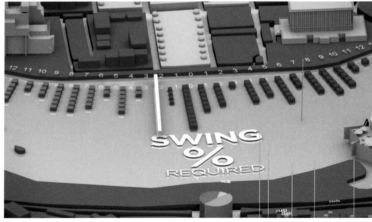

TITLE **THE SEED**

CATEGORY free work

DESIGN Johnny Kelly

DESCRIPTION An epic voyage through nature's life cycle following the trials and tribulations of a humble apple seed.
This clip was made using a mixture of stop motion papercraft and 2-D drawn animation. 23 people were involved in the making and it features a soundtrack by Jape.

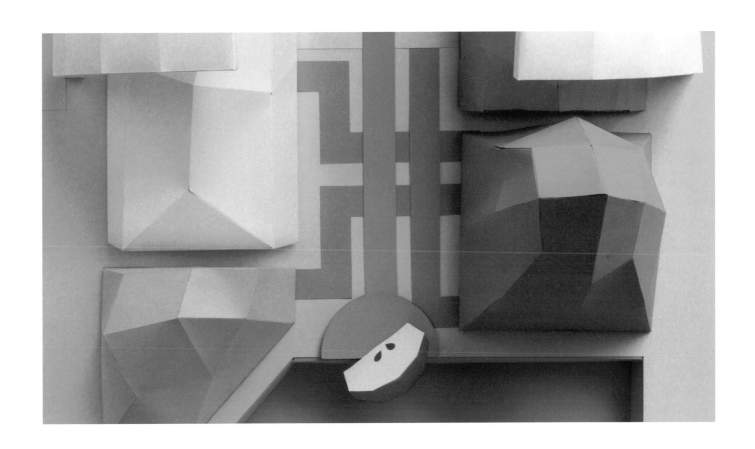

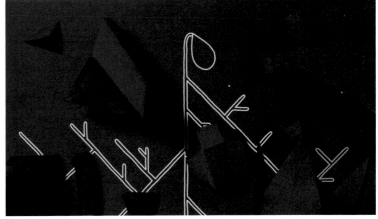

TITLE

BACK TO THE START

CATEGORY   infotainment

CLIENT   Chipotle

STUDIO   CAA and Chipotle

DESCRIPTION   The brief for this film was very open, but the designers were given a comprehensive list of topics and themes to include, i.e. animal welfare, organic farming, the use of antibiotics on livestock, crop rotation, water pollution, and lots of other things that are hard to animate. The biggest challenge was including all of these topics in some form of animated short film without it coming across as a heavy-handed lecture. Chipotle suggested that it have an information graphic feel – like a flow chart – and through careful planning with the previsualization artists at Nexus, it was possible to plan one fluid camera move that would touch on all of these subjects one after another.

TITLE **SUBPRIME**

CATEGORY free work

STUDIO Beeple

DESCRIPTION Watch as the American housing market spirals out of control. An urgent cry for simplicity, *Subprime* uses a constantly rotating isometric perspective to illustrate the current subprime mortgage crisis in the United States. Every successive house that is built folds into itself and sprouts the growth of a bigger one, only to repeat the ultimately futile process again.

BASICS

B1 /
FORMS OF
REPRESENTATION

THE PRESENTATION HAS TO BE CHOSEN KEEPING AN EYE ON THE MESSAGE TO BE COMMUNICATED.

The concept of information graphics covers a broad spectrum of forms of representation. They are broken down into three categories – maps, visual statistics, and representations of principles – and are significant in all disciplines of information graphics, including animated information graphics. This chapter offers insight into the common types of infographic representation.

The borders between the three categories mentioned are fluid. Hence, depending on the context and what the relevant graphic is intended to communicate, combinations of several forms of representation are possible. A common example of this is the distribution of unemployment in a country as illustrated by a thematic map with a regional context. It is a fusion of the elements of visual statistics and cartographic representation. We are introducing here the term *hybrid forms of representation* for such combinations.

The following chapters explain which forms of representation fall under the three higher-level categories of maps, visual statistics, and representations of principles.

B 1.1 / VISUAL STATISTICS

The statistical information graphic is the most common form of representation, along with the cartographic one. We encounter it daily in the mass media, and it is generally known how to read and understand statistical information graphics.

/ ANGELA JANSEN
Handbuch der Infografik,
p. 174

"The main task of a visual statistic is to visualize proportions of quantities." < The designer has three common categories of representation available for this task: bar, line, and pie charts. There are, however, also a number of forms of charts that can scarcely be said to be more common but they are nevertheless clearer, and under certain circumstances they can be employed.

In general, the selection of the chart form must be made keeping an eye on the underlying data set and the corresponding intention to communicate. "In practice, this represents a complex challenge for the information graphic artist, since data sets

/ ANGELA JANSEN
Handbuch der Infografik,
p. 174

can usually be converted into several chart forms." < Depending on the complexity of the data set, moreover, it is possible to combine different chart forms to provide the viewer with more detailed information. The degree of complexity that can be communicated depends considerably on the context and medium in which the visual statistic is placed. For example, the viewer of an animated information graphic has only a limited time available in the passive moving image, and the designer

/ B 5.3
THE LIMITS OF THE
PASSIVE MOVING IMAGE

must consider whether the relevant content can be absorbed in that time frame. < On the other hand, the moving image also offers the possibility of dividing the information it contains sequentially and introducing it gradually with the aid

/ C2
ANIMATION

of an animation. < Thus the viewer's absorption of the information is guided, ultimately providing the viewer with a familiar overview of the graphic and making relevant comparisons possible.

Statistical information graphics represent a broad field of expertise, both in terms of complexity and the variety of possible visualizations. This study is limited in scope, so it can only give a glimpse here. A more detailed theoretical discussion is part of the work of, amongst others, EDWARD R. TUFTE.

B 1.1.1 / PIE CHARTS

The pie chart represents the whole and its constituent parts, allowing for a comparison of the corresponding relations. > **FIG. 1**

B 1.1.2 / BAR CHARTS

Bar charts are used to compare different kinds of data and to emphasize the proportion of subsets to one another. > **FIGS. 2 & 3**

Their bars can be horizontally or vertically aligned. A common example for the use of bar charts is the visual representation of price activity over a given period of time that intends to illustrate possible trends and patterns. It is very useful if one is trying to record certain information, whether it is continuous or non-continuous data.

B 1.1.3 / LINE AND AREA CHARTS

Information graphics that aim to demonstrate the development of multiple values in detail should make use of a line or area chart. The representation of stockprices is probably the most prominent example of these forms of charts. The decision whether to use a line or area chart should be based on the content that is to be visualized. "The curve chart represents abstract numbers (imagine a 'fever curve'), while the area chart depicts real matter (imagine a 'stack')." < > **FIG. 4**

/ ANGELA JANSEN
Handbuch der Infografik,
p. 184

FIG. 1
Pie chart, depicting the whole and its percentages as subsections.

FIGS. 2 & 3
Here subsets are compared by lining them up on a baseline.

FIG. 4
This chart shows the precise temporal development of two values.

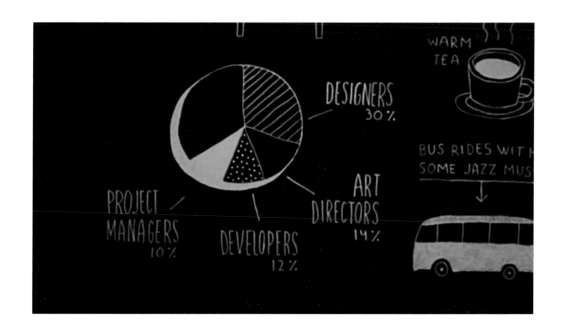

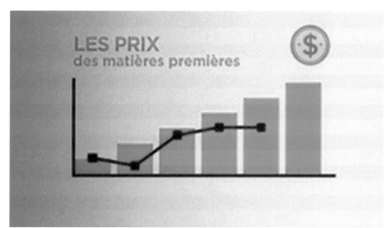

FIG. 2

FIG. 3

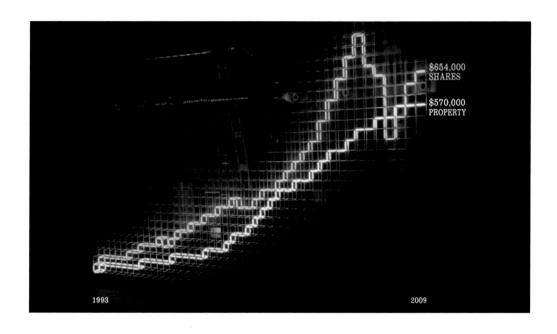

DISPLAY PATTERNS
FOR VISUAL STATISTICS

CORRELATIONS

Scatterplot

Bubble Chart

CONTINUOUS QUANTITIES

Simple
Line Chart

Multiset
Line Chart

Stacked
Area Chart

Sparklines

DISCRETE QUANTITIES

Simple
Bar Chart

Multiset
Bar Chart

Dot Matrix

Stacked
Bar Chart

Isometric
Bar Chart

Span Chart

OVERVIEW OF DISPLAY PATTERNS
FROM CHRISTIAN BEHRENS'S MASTER'S THESIS
"The Form of Facts and Figures:
Design Patterns for Interactive Visualizations"
www.niceone.org > PDF p. 37

PROPORTIONS

Simple
Pie Chart

Ring Chart

FLOWS

Sankey
Diagram

Thread Arcs

HIERARCHIES

Tree Diagram

Treemap

NETWORKS

Tree Diagram

Relation Circle

Pearl Necklace

SPACE

Topographic
Map

Thematic
Map

B 1.2 / SCHEMATIC DIAGRAMS

Schematic diagrams are employed when depicting the precise structure of an object, complex connections, or abstract processes. "The spectrum is broad: from the sketch of a company's structure (the classic organizational chart) to the diagram of how a technical installation functions." < Schematic diagrams are often found in instruction manuals, advertisements, and teaching contexts. In science and research, they illustrate theories and make them accessible to a wide audience. In short, the schematic drawing is employed where the limits of the real picture and verbal description are reached.

JANSEN divides the forms of schematic drawing into images of content and structure, and process graphics. What follows here is a brief overview of their respective characteristics and the possibilities for employing them.

B 1.2.1 / IMAGES OF CONTENT

"Images of content are intended not just to show the viewer an object but also to permit insight into it by means of skilled didactic treatment." < Hence the content image serves the detailed description of an object, e.g., in the context of an instruction manual. > FIG. 5 Its depiction should be based as closely as possible on the real model, since a high degree of recognizability will improve the viewer's understanding. This does not, however, mean it should be illustrated in a photorealistic way, since an image of content should be limited to the details necessary to convey the information, which demands a certain degree of abstraction. < "If only a superficial understanding needs to be communicated, simplified and reduced representation of the object is appropriate." <

Conversely, the more complex the understanding to be communicated, the more detailed the model. The complexity of content image should also be based on its target audience. An audience of specialists can be expected to cope with higher information density than someone unfamiliar with the field could.

B 1.2.2 / CROSS SECTION

The cross section offers a view inside an object, enabling the viewer to learn about its structure or internal processes. The rendering can be two or three dimensional; the latter is particularly appropriate for unfamiliar objects, for which a 2-D drawing is often too abstract.

It should also be noted that a cutaway section must be distinguished clearly from the rest of the graphic – for example, by the use of color – and the position of the cutaway should not make it more difficult to perceive the form of the whole. > FIG. 6

/ ANGELA JANSEN
Handbuch der Infografik,
p. 116

/ ANGELA JANSEN
Handbuch der Infografik,
p. 118

/ B 3.5
REDUCTION

/ ANGELA JANSEN
Handbuch der Infografik,
p. 118

FIG. 5
This example gives an overview of the detailed construction of a satellite.

FIG. 6
These cross sections give the viewer a look at the interior of the object.

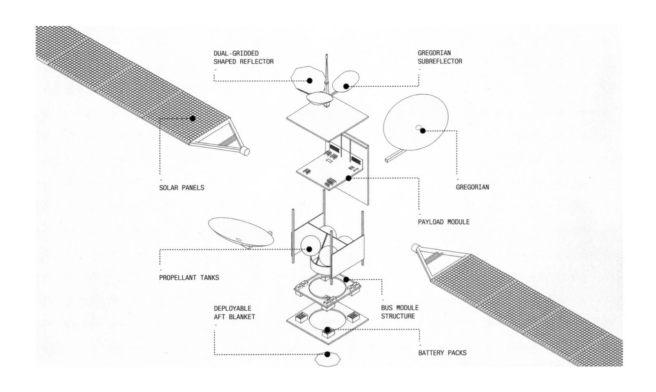

DUAL-GRIDDED
SHAPED REFLECTOR

GREGORIAN
SUBREFLECTOR

SOLAR PANELS

GREGORIAN

PAYLOAD MODULE

PROPELLANT TANKS

DEPLOYABLE
AFT BLANKET

BUS MODULE
STRUCTURE

BATTERY PACKS

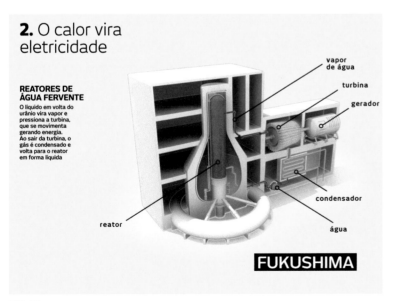

2. O calor vira eletricidade

REATORES DE ÁGUA FERVENTE

O líquido em volta do urânio vira vapor e pressiona a turbina, que se movimenta gerando energia. Ao sair da turbina, o gás é condensado e volta para o reator em forma líquida

vapor de água

turbina

gerador

condensador

reator

água

FUKUSHIMA

FIG. 6A

HOW THE ESCALATOR WORKS

ASSEMBLY
FIGURE 14-3
Schindler Group

FIG. 6B

B 1.2.3 / VISUALIZATIONS

The most familiar form of visualization is the organizational chart. It provides information about the hierarchical relationships within a certain group. Images of structure generally serve to visualize abstract processes, such as the fluctuation of financial resources between banks. In that case, it can be useful to employ a visual, symbolic metaphor to clarify the context of the graphic and rouse the viewer's interest. For example, bank accounts can be represented by piggy banks, making the graphic more inviting without changing the content. It is important that the metaphor be appropriate to the statement and familiar to the target audience for the graphic to avoid misunderstandings. > FIG. 7

B 1.2.4 / PROCESS GRAPHICS

The process graphic depicts a dynamic process. Depending on the complexity of the latter, it may have to be reduced to the components that are relevant to communicating insight. This is also reflected in the depiction. JANSEN explains by using the example of depicting a technical process: "The process graphic had to depict the process in a comprehensible way, but without aspiring to meeting the requirement that a function machine could be built based on the drawing." < Processes can be visualized by means of an overall image or by a series of images. Series of images – that is, several individual images – offer more room for specific details within the process, but also make it more difficult to perceive the overall context.

The overall image, the sequence of images, and the feature graphic are subcategories of the process graphic.

The overall image "can clarify political decisions or technical process – if it clearly leads the viewer's eye through the process." < In order to guide the viewer's eye in this way, it is necessary to structure the overall image to be read from top left to bottom right. A clear organization is also necessary. > FIG. 8

In addition, the visual aspects of the process have to be clearly distinct and the elements that logically belong together must be recognizable as such.

"Sequences of images direct the eye to selected steps, and not so much to the overall context." < The recognizability of the individual images is more important than formal variety. For example, perspectives and the colors of the individual elements must be retained through the entire sequence. The significant components have to be introduced in the first image of the sequence. This increases the viewer's attention, enabling him or her to concentrate more on the relationships between the elements when viewing the subsequent images in the sequence.

The feature graphic illustrates complex connections such as sequences of movements, instruction manuals, or diagrams.

/ ANGELA JANSEN
Handbuch der Infografik,
p. 132

/ ANGELA JANSEN
Handbuch der Infografik,
p. 136

/ ANGELA JANSEN
Handbuch der Infografik,
p. 136

FIG. 7
Organizational chart

FIG. 8
Here the winners' paths are traced from the qualifying rounds to the presentation ceremony.

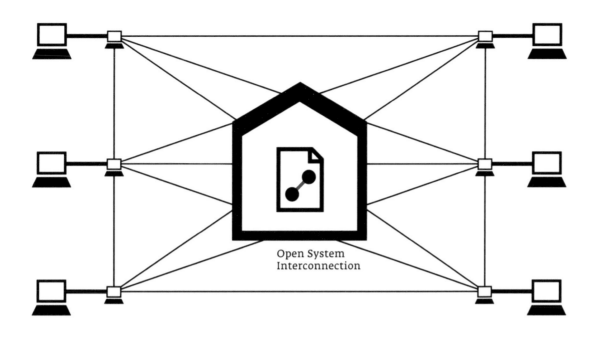

Open System
Interconnection

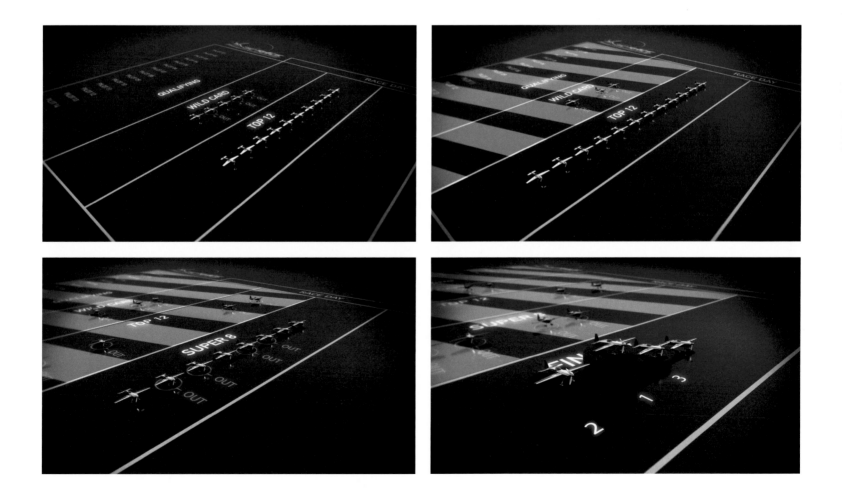

B 1.3 / MAPS

Cartographic information graphics make it possible to absorb information quickly and are therefore, in contrast to ordinary maps, limited to depicting essential components that contribute to understanding.

/ "Unlike a map, the form and content of a cartographic information graphic are created to communicate spatially a specific, current piece of information; it is not produced for a general purpose or overarching theme." <

/ WOLFGANG SCHARFE
Handbuch der Infografik,
p. 142

The graphic merely depicts the relevant activity space. Because it is usually just a small detail of a region, a country, or the world, it should be supplemented by another map that offers an overview of the corresponding larger area. That way the overall context remains apparent to the viewer. In addition, in order to make it easy to understand, all the elements of the cartographic infographic should be labeled. To that end we will examine in greater detail the correct labeling of information graphics in section B 3.3.2 "Line Charts."

B 1.3.1 / MAPS OF EVENT SPACES

The form of representation is based on the principle of a topographic map[1] and describes the spatial circumstances of an event – an accident or an act of war, for example. "In each case it is necessary to emphasize in a graphically concise manner the place or spaces of the event within the map's event space." < To simplify the viewer's assessment of the space, prominent points in the surroundings, such as bodies of water or surrounding countries, should be clearly labeled. <> **FIGS. 9 & 10**

/ WOLFGANG SCHARFE
Handbuch der Infografik,
p. 148

/ B 3.2.2
LABELING ALL
THE ELEMENTS

B 1.3.2 / THEMATIC MAPS

The thematic map provides information about the spatial distribution of one or more phenomena within a specific thematic complex. For example, it can provide information about the location of production sites. This method is often used to link geographical and statistical information, such as the global fischeries exploitation. > **FIG. 10** Depending on the number of phenomena, usually different symbols are used to mark the space, and they have to be explained in an accompanying legend. It is not generally advisable to use a permanent legend in an animated information graphic, since this forces the viewer to jump back and forth between the graphic and the legend. This takes up valuable time, which one cannot always afford.

---

1   The topographic map is a large- to medium-scale map on which geographical objects – that is, the visible objects and circumstances of the surface of earth, especially terrain formations – are depicted according to scale in their correct position and in their entirety, based on a system of cartographic symbols.

FIG. 9
A second map shows a detail of the first. The red arrow indicates movement between two points.

FIG. 10
This thematic map shows the course of the nineteenth stage of the Tour de France.

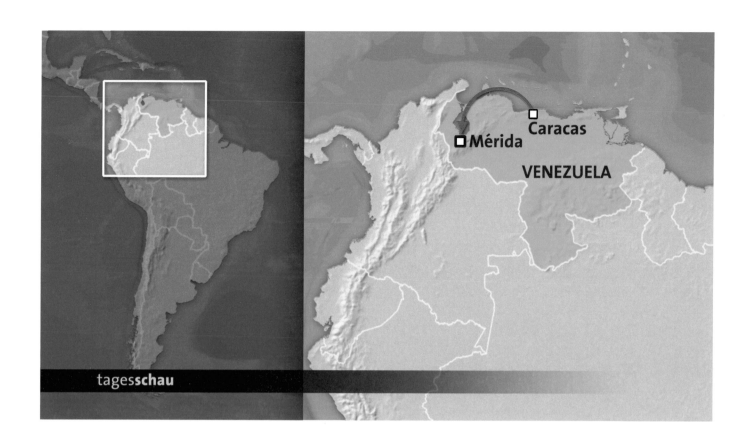

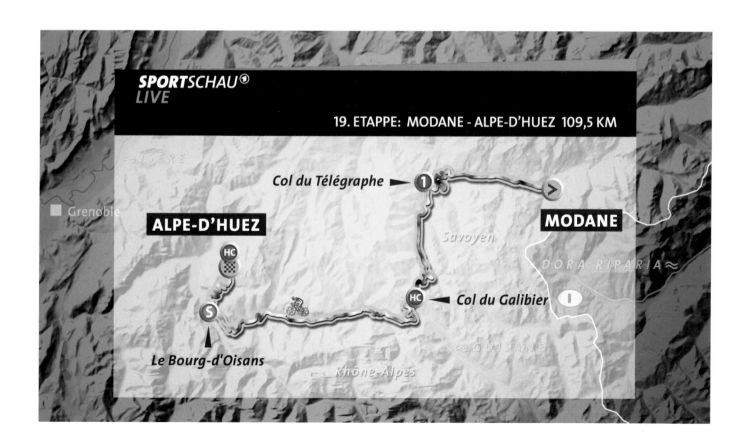

/ B 3.2
LABELING
/ C 3
VOICE OVER

Hence it should be avoided wherever possible, either by a label < in the graphic or a mention in the voice over. <

Because the passive moving image is subject to a linear structure, offers a limited area for representation, and ties the viewer to a defined time frame, captions are less suitable here. The risk that the viewer will lose information when looking back and forth between the caption and the graphic is too great and should be avoided. One possibility, however, is to introduce the relevant symbols by means of a caption that appears briefly and then fades out again. This approach presumes that the viewer has been following the representation from the beginning, otherwise valuable information will be lost.

B 1.3.3 / WEATHER MAPS

Because they are so widely disseminated, weather maps occupy a special place among thematic maps. Technical advances have improved their design. > **FIGS. 11 & 12**

/ WOLFGANG SCHARFE
Handbuch der Infografik,
p. 160

/ "From the mid-1980s to the early 1990s, there was a transformation from the "meteorological" weather map to the "visual" map: weather maps increased in size; satellite images were added; and fronts and isobars were replaced by graphic symbols for sun and clouds." <

It has become quite common to show related information, such as pollen counts, alongside weather reports.

FIG. 11
Thematic map showing global fishing.

FIG. 12
Weather map with overview of temperatures.

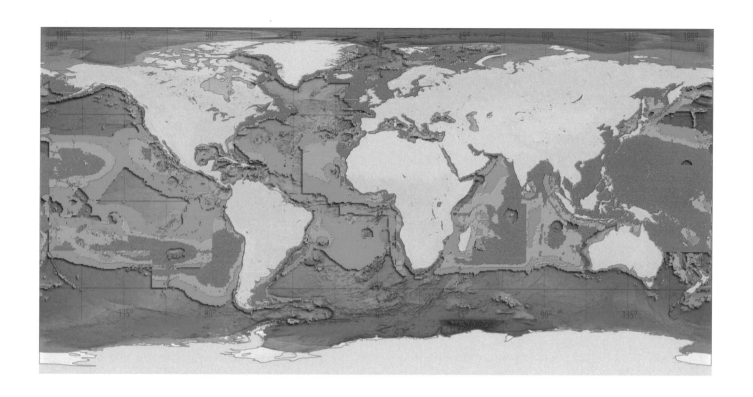

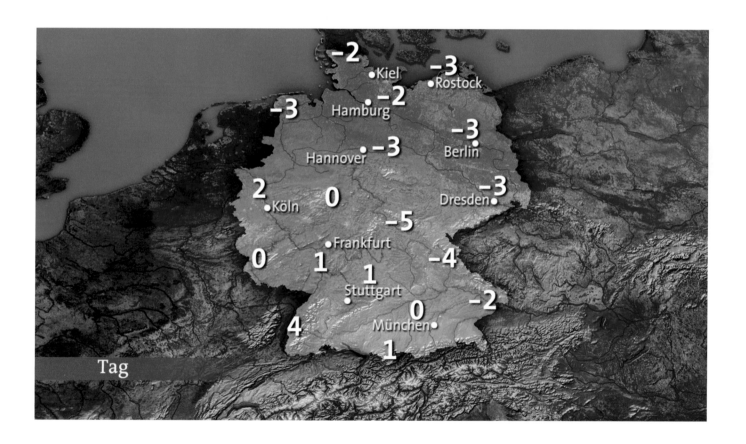

B2 /
PERCEPTION

AN OBJECT IS NEVER JUST SEEN: THE VIEWER'S SURROUND-INGS, TIME AND SITE, EVENTS AND STATES OF MIND ALWAYS PLAY A ROLE.

In order to design information in such a way that it can be absorbed despite the limitations of our sense organs, every designer concerned with communicating specific content and especially communicating information should know the principles of and ideas behind the psychology of perception and consciously apply them in his or her work. In this chapter we explain what the principles are and why they are so important.

Perception generally refers to the sensory awareness of physical stimuli coming from creature's outside world.

This means the conscious and unconscious collection of information via the senses. The information received and evaluated in this way becomes perceptions, also known as percepts. An object is never just seen: the viewer's surroundings, time and place, events and states of mind always play a role in his or her perceptions as well. The information is constantly compared to constructs or schemas stored as part of one's inner world of ideas.

B 2.1 / THEORIES OF PERCEPTION

The psychology of perception developed four theories of perception for the practice of visual communication in the previous century:

/ theory of expectation,
/ theory of structure,
/ theory of empathy, and
/ Gestalt theory.

The theory of expectation and Gestalt theory are particularly relevant to the design of animated information graphics.

B 2.1.1 / THEORY OF EXPECTATION

The theory of expectation says that perception signifies the selection of the environment according to a pattern of expectations: people must be willing to perceive, otherwise they will not consciously perceive – that is, they do not direct their attention to the stimulus in question. In short, people only see what they want to see; what they don't want to see, they don't see. When opinions change, perception changes.

One clear example of that: If a man goes to the supermarket because he has run out of tomatoes, and goes to the supermarket solely to buy more, he will only have eyes for red, juicy tomatoes. He will be indifferent to everything else as long as no more powerful visual stimulus distracts him from his task.

In addition, knowledge can influence one's willingness to perceive and the act of perception itself. For example, certain phenomena that occur in the relevant spatial and temporal context are expected in advance but by perceptive cells that are not activated: When something is perceived, attracting attention, the gaze turns to it

/ C 2.3
FORMS

and its contours are fed into the recognition of form. <

The designer's approach to information graphics with moving images and content should consider how to work out patterns of expectation and possibilities for directing attention in order to choose the design elements and forms of representation accordingly. An understanding of the target audience's previous knowledge and media competence should be developed.

B 2.1.2 / GESTALT THEORY

A *gestalt* is a group of elements in which the whole is more than the sum of its parts. For example, the elements in FIG. 1 are perceived not as two dots, a line, a circle, and a surface but as a unity – a gestalt.

The elements are related to one another, adding to their meaning in a way that goes

/ B 2.2.5
THE LAW OF
ÜBERSUMMENHAFTIGKEIT

beyond the original information. <

Images of objects are not seen as they are but rather as they are recreated as gestalt images through the effect of the laws of organization.

FIG. 1

B 2.2 / THE GESTALT LAWS

Gestalt theory, which is still relevant today to artistic creative design, was developed in the early twentieth century by the Berlin school of Gestalt psychology, which included MAX WERTHEIMER, WOLFGANG KÖHLER, KURT LEWIN, and KURT GOLDSTEIN, among others. < Gestalt theory states that during visual perception, model-like images – known as Gestalt images – are produced in the brain.

gestalttherapie-lexikon.de/
gestaltpsychologie.htm

Gestalt theorists developed more than a hundred Gestalt laws, all of which have one essence in common: simple, economic forms are perceived preferentially.

The Gestalt laws play an important role in visual and acoustic perception. For example, they are employed by scientists working on artificial intelligence to develop computer programs designed for pattern and object recognition. Their use in software-ergonomic developments for user interfaces is aimed at creating clear and well-structured interfaces.

The organizing effect of the Gestalt laws can help designers create exciting and lively representations. Often the eye feels magically attracted to depictions produced by observing the Gestalt laws.

The challenge of information graphics is to convey concrete material in such a way that is clearly perceivable. Because of the time constraints that result from a moving image, designers must produce a deliberate and precise design. Such a design can be achieved with the aid of the Gestalt laws. <

Only the most important Gestalt laws are discussed here.

/ BIRGIT GURTNER, KARIN
KAINEDER, HEIKE SPERLING:
Reduktion, Interaktion,
Bewegtbild

B 2.2.1 / THE LAW OF *PRÄGNANZ* (PRECISION)

A gestalt with precise and clearly distinguishable features is perceived preferentially, more easily recognized, and better remembered. Gestalt theory regards this law as a basic principle of perception and derives the Law of Good Gestalt from it. In FIG. 2, we perceive a circle and a rectangle at an angle, lying over the circle. Our brain relies on its previous experience and fills in the missing parts of both surfaces. This example shows that simple, familiar forms can be more easily remembered and processed more quickly. When creating information graphics with moving images, it is therefore advantageous to choose a clear and unambiguous formal idiom.
> FIG. 2

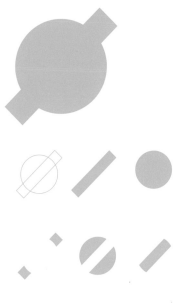

FIG. 2

B 2.2.2 / THE LAW OF GOOD GESTALT

Good gestalts are memorable and precise. They are therefore easier to remember than gestalts characterized by disorder and randomness. If forms are based on basic shapes such as the circle, square, and triangle – that is, on fundamental geometric shapes – as a rule they will have good gestalt. > FIG. 3

The more simply a form is defined geometrically, the more it will strive to be isolated optically. / Axel Seyler

The Law of Precision and the Law of Good Gestalt are probably the most important laws when developing animated information graphics. Their goal is to reduce the diversity of forms – that is, visual abstraction – creating signs that can be perceived quickly while at the same time restricting the interpretive latitude as much as possible. In the medium of the moving image, these principles become even more important since the transience of the medium leaves the viewer less time to recognize the form.

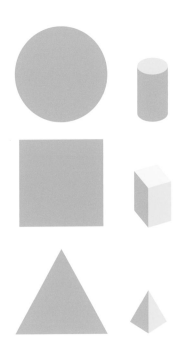

FIG. 3

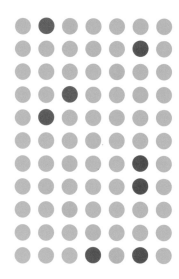

B 2.2.3 / THE LAW OF SYMMETRY

Symmetrical forms are perceived preferentially and integrated into units. If both symmetrical and asymmetrical forms are present, the symmetrical structures will will come to the foreground as a figure and the asymmetrically arranged elements will appear to be the background.

In FIG. 4, the pink dots constitute a zigzag form and thus move into the foreground. The blue and gray dots do not form a figure and thus become the background.

B 2.2.4 / THE LAW OF PROXIMITY

Elements that lie short distances from one another are perceived as belonging together. The spatial proximity thus leads to the elements being combined and produces connections. > FIG. 5

The significance of this for information design is that the individual elements of a graphic can be integrated into units of sense or that their connection in terms of content can be maintained by means of corresponding position. For example, labels should be positioned close to the corresponding element.

In general, however, it must be kept in mind that elements with very different formal, optical features – e.g., form and color – can be understood as separated in terms of content even when immediately adjacent. <

/ B 2.2.7
THE LAW OF SIMILARITY

The Law of Closure can be derived from the Law of Proximity: elements lying closely together will be combined into an optical series.

FIG. 4

B 2.2.5 / THE LAW OF *ÜBERSUMMENHAFTIGKEIT* (WHOLE MORE THAN SUM OF PARTS)

The designed whole is more than the sum of its parts. Hence a square is a square, while many squares are not necessarily many squares but can add up to produce a figure. In their totality, the partial elements become more significant than the sum of the parts. > FIG. 6

In a multimedia context, the sum can only exceed the parts when the components (audio, sound, voice over, graphic) are related. Hence it can be perceived as very disturbing when the audio event does not establish a relationship to the content, for example.

FIG. 5

B 2.2.6 / THE FIGURE-GROUND PRINCIPLE

Already in an early stage of the perception process, there is a separation of the objects (or figures) in the foreground and the background. An object can be emphasized against its background by various features, including color, brightness, or movement. As soon as this separation takes place, the visual system can devote itself to the foreground and hence to object recognition. Everything that is seen is always divided into foreground and background. As FIG. 7 shows, it is impossible to see two forms at the same time. Either one sees the vase or the faces. <

/ ROLAND MANGOLD:
Informationspsychologie,
p. 100

FIG.6

B 2.2 / THE GESTALT LAWS

FIG. 7

This is an elementary fact for the design of information graphics.

An inadequate separation of foreground and background impedes the understanding of the object, since even elements that have no significance demand the viewer's attention. Freely adapting the principle that form follows function, designers must pay particular attention to this fact when designing.

B 2.2.7 / THE LAW OF SIMILARITY

Similar elements are perceived as belonging more closely together than different ones. Grouping by similarity is more dominant than by proximity. Objects that belong together based on form should therefore be integrated not just spatially but also formally and optically. Formal and optical variables include form, color, brightness, size, and direction, with color dominating the other variables in keeping with the psychology of perceptual cognition. > FIG. 8

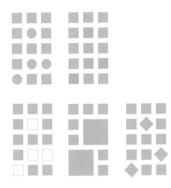

FIG. 8

B 2.2.8 / THE LAW OF CONTINUITY

Elements that represent a spatial or temporal continuation of previous elements or are arranged in a simple, regular, or harmonious continuity will be perceived as belonging together, i.e., as a figure or a unity. > FIG. 9

This law can also be applied to auditory signals. Thus tones can be perceived together after an interruption.

The Law of Common Fate follows the Law of Continuity. Elements that experience a similar development or change are perceived by the viewer as belonging together. For example, the ways individual objects are animated can contribute to their grouping.

FIG. 9

B 2.2.9 / THE LAW OF CLOSURE

Elements lined up can be perceived as belonging together. This gives the impression of a closed form. Something that is not present is supplied by the perceptual system. > FIG. 10

Our brain is constantly searching for patterns. This fact underscores the importance of the visual techniques identified here. Even if the laws may at first glance seem trivial or obvious to every designer, they are often disregarded. In the case of the passive moving image in particular, when the viewer is subjected to a fixed temporal sequence, one must have a very rapid and easily perceptible visualization, clearly focused on the information to be conveyed. The gestalt laws can be very useful in achieving this.

With information graphics in moving images, the whole is not just the sum of the individual elements in the image, but also the sum that takes into account cinematic aspects such as the movement, development, and changes of these elements over time. The distant becomes close, different elements become similar, individual parts become an overall picture.

FIG. 10

B3 /
CONTENT

A GOOD INFORMATION GRAPHIC MAKES ITS CONTENT, OR ITS ESSENCE, AS ACCESSIBLE AS POSSIBLE IN A BRIEF PERIOD OF TIME.

In order to preserve the seriousness of the data underlying an information graphic, it is important to keep it transparent and to respect basic rules when translating it. The following chapter will explain in detail which rules promote this.

B 3.1 / CORE MESSAGE

Despite the many theories about the implementation and design of information graphics, all the approaches that form the theoretical basis for the present book have one principle in common:

A good information graphic makes its content, or its essence, as accessible as possible in a brief period of time.

This was already expressed by OTTO NEURATH in his Viennese Method: "An image produced in accordance with the rules of the Viennese Method reveals at first glance the most important thing about the object." < In their defintions of an information graphic, JACQUES BERTIN and ANGELA JANSEN also advocate this standpoint: "The meaningful visual form, perceptible in the minimum instant of vision, will be called the IMAGE." < "Information graphics present complex facts synoptically – that is to say, at a glance." < These principles can be summed up by the demand that there be a transparent core message. Graphic reduction is a basic requirement to that end. This means above all that every element in an information graphic conveys meaning and will be seen separately from components of a purely aesthetic nature. < An appealing design that will grab the viewer's attention and awaken his or her interest in the content presented is, of course, also important and necessary. But the design should not overlap the information to the extent that the latter becomes illegible or difficult to extract. There is, therefore, a clear hierarchy: first the information, then the graphic design. EDWARD R. TUFTE goes even farther with regard to the design of statistical graphics. "All graphic elements in an information graphic convey information; everything else is superfluous." <

TUFTE introduced the term *chartjunk*[1] for redundant elements in a graphic and stated that the viewer should concentrate entirely on the data and content of the graphic. Graphic reduction is also eminently important for a moving image, since the sequence limits the time in which individual elements can be perceived.

/ FRANK HARTMANN,
ERWIN K. BAUER:
Bildersprache,
p. 10

/ JACQUES BERTIN:
Semiology of Graphics,
p. 142
/ ANGELA JANSEN,
WOLFGANG SCHARFE:
Handbuch der Infografik,
Preface

/ JACQUES :
Semiology of Graphics,
p. 142

/ ANGELA JANSEN:
Handbuch der Infografik,
p. 90

---

1 *Chartjunk* refers to all visual elements in charts and graphs that are not necessary to comprehend the information represented on the graph, or that distract the viewer from this information.

/ C 1
NARRATION

/ B 2
PERCEPTION
/ C 2.1
COLORS
/ C 2.3
FORMS

Thus it is necessary to consider precisely which elements should be the focus of a narrative sequence of images and when in order to convey the core message. ‹ Finally, it should be mentioned that when formulating a core message graphic, not only reduction but nearly all the factors – from aspects of the psychology of perception to the means of design – play a role. ‹ Ultimately, its effectiveness depends on the correct employment of all available means.

B 3.2 / LABELING

B 3.2.1 / HEADING

/ B 3.1
CORE MESSAGE

As mentioned above in the context of the core message, the content of an information graphic should be evident at first glance. ‹ This goal can be achieved by a clear, reduced design, on the one hand, and by an expressing a heading, on the other. The heading must give the viewer the opportunity to grasp the theme of the graphic. This is especially true when the context is not evident from the graphic alone. For example, the meaning of a pie chart will scarcely be evident without clear labeling.

Above all, a heading should be succinctly formulated.

/ B 3.4
MANIPULATING DATA

To that end, there are two possibilities when formulating it: either the author just identifies the theme (e.g., "Sales of Company X in 2009") and leaves it to the audience to derive the message's tendency from the graphic. Or it already underscores the main message (e.g., "Double-Digit Growth in the Electronics Sector"), which the viewer then finds confirmed in the graphic. The first, objective variant can lead to a more precise engagement on the part of the viewer, as long as he or she is not frightened off by the need to further decode the data. The second, evaluative variant may shorten the time necessary to perceive it but it also anticipates the insight and leaves room for manipulations. ‹ In general, it should be said here that, as necessary as objectivity may be, the heading also has to attract interest and should make the viewer curious about the information depicted. For example, the heading "Semiconductors Are the New Gold" also permits inferences about the main message, but without coming across as dry or boring. In the case of a moving image, headings are not treated very rigorously. A formal analysis of 149 animated information graphics from German news and science broadcasts on television showed that the majority of graphics did not use a heading at all.

/ C 3
VOICE OVER

This is often because the speaker (the voice over) takes over the function of a heading. ‹ The disadvantage of this, however, is that the subject of the graphic is no longer visible after it has been identified by the speaker. At least in the case of longer reports, this can make it more difficult to understand the graphic, since the viewer cannot easily join in at a later point. In the case of longer sequences with animated information graphics, it makes sense to subdivide the theme into several logical subthemes and to give each a corresponding heading.

B 3.2.2 / LABELING ALL THE ELEMENTS

Along with the heading, the labeling of the graphic elements used is an important aspect of an information graphic. The full content of the information is revealed only through it. In this context, several guidelines should be observed, which will be explained in greater detail below. The Law of Proximity describes the necessity to keep the label of each individual graphic element inside the graphic whenever possible. ‹ This is particularly true for the use of cartographic depictions and schematic diagrams, but when labeling graphs it is advisable to mark the graph itself to promote rapid understanding. COLIN WARE, the director of the Data Visualization Research Labs at the University of New Hampshire, identifies three possibilities for internal labeling (static links) that are relevant in the context of information graphics: ‹

/ B 2.2.4
LAW OF PROXIMITY

/ COLIN WARE:
Visual Thinking for Design,
p. 323

/ **1. Proximity** > The label near the relevant element. > FIG. 1
/ **2. Continuity/connectedness** > Label and element connected by a line. > FIG. 2
/ **3. Common region** > Label and element are bordered by a line. > FIG. 3

The technical conditions of a moving image generally necessitate larger labels, which in turn take up more space in the area available for depiction. Connecting via a line often frees up the necessary space when several labels are necessary in one area. If there are many elements to be labeled, labeling within the graphic can reduce legibility. Here it is advisable to use a legend and place the labeling consistent outside the graphic. This approach has the disadvantage that the viewer has to leap back and forth between the graphic and the legend. ‹ This slows perception and hence is ill-suited to a time-dependent medium such as the moving image. Such an application suggests a sequential division of the information into small units with labels inside each partial graphic. ‹ Another option is labeling with a speaker's comments (voice over), ‹ thus relieving the burden on the visual aspect of the graphic. In combination with so-called stimulus guides, the viewer can be pointed toward the relevant part within an established sequence. ‹

/ C 5.1
LEAPS OF THE EYE

/ C 1
NARRATION
/ C 3
VOICE OVER

/ C 5
FOCUSING THE
VIEWER'S ATTENTION

FIG. 1

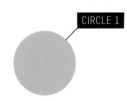

FIG. 2

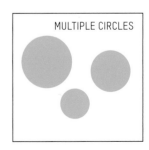

FIG. 3

B 3.2.3 / SERIOUSNESS

Data presented by an information graphic usually convey a reliable and serious impression. The scientific look of visual statistics supports this assumption. The viewer, however, often has no opportunity to test the accuracy of the data represented.

Analyses of information graphics used on German news broadcasts have shown that three-quarters of the reports that employ visual statistics did not identify a source for the data or poll numbers.

/ B 3.4
MANIPULATING DATA

Sources belong in any information graphic that is to be taken seriously and there is no reason to be shy of the data it contains being tested. Conversely, suppressing the source of statistical data can be understood as an instrument of manipulation when designing information graphics. Additional information on the potential of information graphics to manipulate and on the importance of properly representing data can be found elsewhere in this volume. ‹ If limited space makes it impossible to include the sources of the data in a moving image or on a chart, it is often possible to include it in a credit sequence. Another important point in this context: cartographic depictions should always indicate their scale to give the viewer a picture of the dimensions. This is unnecessary only in the case of world maps.

B 3.3 / LEGIBILITY OF CHARTS

In order to make charts as legible as possible, it is necessary to observe several rudimentary principles that have proven effective in print designs of information graphics. They are, however, of only limited validity for moving images because the basic conditions are different.

B 3.3.1 / BAR CHARTS

To make a comparison of the subsets easier within a bar chart, the bars should have a common baseline. The intent to communicate should define its graphic representation: values that change over time should be shown by rows, temporal series by vertical bars. The viewer is accustomed to seeing the time axis oriented horizontally, and hence it should always be employed that way. The use of horizontal bars can in some cases have the advantage that relatively large labels can be placed underneath the graphic or inside the bars.

Drastic differences in the expression of individual parts as numbers can exceed the limits of the size of the graphic or the intended layout. When that happens, the format of the graphic has to be adjusted. Simply lopping off the elements, and labeling them accordingly, would distort the overall look of the graphic. "This would ignore the basic task of a visual statistic – namely, showing the difference in meaning as a visual difference." < Such distortion can also be caused by excessive use of perspective. That is one reason to use isometric representations, since they do not distort the quantities. FIG. 4 is thus a legitimate design possibility, but in TUFTE's view it should be regarded as redundant.

/ ANGELA JANSEN
Handbuch der Infografik,
p. 180

In lieu of bars, the proportion of subsets to one another can also be represented by symbols. The images developed by OTTO NEURATH are based on this procedure. A symbol takes on a certain numeric value and its repetition illustrates the total quantity. The juxtaposition of different symbols of various numbers provides a striking visual comparison and hence a quick overview. The specific value of a quantity is revealed only by a second step, since the viewer has to ascertain the number of symbols and calculate their value.

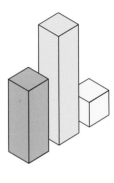

FIG. 4

/ "In bar charts, the gaps between the bars should be about half the size of the width of one bar. It is also advisable to make the longest bar about ten times as long as it is wide." < > **FIG. 5**

/ RICHARD E. MAYER:
Multimedia Learning,
p. 180

However, some situations necessitate making the gaps much smaller. For example, if it is necessary to view a hundred bars side by side in order to interpret a trend, larger gaps between bars should be avoided.

"Bar charts should show at least four and at most 12 bars." < When choosing this number, one should, however, also consider what one intends to convey. If the point is to show a trend or a value within a span of time, and each individual value is not important, then it is certainly conceivable to have more than 12 bars. Given the temporal aspect of a moving image, the simultaneous perception of charts with twelve bars requires an attention span unusual for this medium. Even if the viewer is led through the graphic by building it up sequentially – e.g., by fading the bars in one at a time – the final examination of the overall pictures and the formation of comparisons takes more time.

/ MARTIN LIEBIG:
Die Infografik,
p. 306

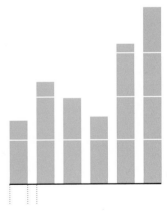

FIG. 5

B 3.3.2 / LINE CHARTS

In everyday use of these chart forms, we observe the representation cut by the zero line. Apart from purely pragmatic reasons such as better use of the format, this usually serves to dramatize the values shown. Although it can still be described as a true representation, it conveys a false impression if the viewer does not study the graphic sufficiently.

The zero line need not be drawn at all. It can also be determined by the background of the graphic. In his remarks on the subject of graphical excellence, TUFTE also dispenses with representing the zero line. It should also be noted that average values, such as annual production of cars, cannot be represented as line or area charts, since an interpolated continuity is produced that does not suit the actual development.

/ DER AUER GRAFIKDIENST:
*Infografik:
Die optische Sprache,*
p. 10

"A line chart should show no more than five curves. If more than five comparisons are necessary, it is better to have several line charts side by side." < When employing a line chart with five curves, the designer should be aware of the aforementioned short time span of the moving medium. It depends on the information to be presented. For example, if the point is to show a sudden fall in the price of an automobile manufacturer's stock compared to four of its competitors, a voice over can refer to this circumstance in order to guide the viewer at a certain time. Much like with the aforementioned intended message of bar charts, here too the designer would like to show a trend or a comparison of a number of values, so it becomes possible to display more than five lines.

B 3.3.3 / PIE CHARTS

Following the Law of Conventions, the literature often advises place as the most important value at top center in the so-called twelve o'clock position of the circle. The other values should follow clockwise from there in order of importance or size. This approach can be applied without restriction to a moving image. "It is usually recommended that a pie chart consist of three to eight segments." < The restrictions noted in the context of the number of elements used in line charts apply here too. Beyond that, a pie chart has to equal 100 percent. It should have no more than six parts, since smaller differences in size make it more difficult to compare and make the graphic more difficult to read. Another thing to keep in mind with regard to legibility is the distortion of a pie chart caused, for example, by its perspectival arrangement in space. In general, we advise against such distortions, since their optical feedback represents an unnecessary task for the viewer and slows the process of perception. Moreover, elements located in the foreground of the perspective are given greater importance, which can also lead to distortion of their true content.

/ HANNO SPRISSLER:
Infografiken gestalten,
p. 35

As an alternative to the pie chart, the proportion of subsets to the whole can also be represented using other elementary geometric forms such as the rectangle. All the elements must have the same elementary form – in this case, a rectangle. Different forms are difficult to compare because their surface area varies.

Finally, we should note that highly complex charts are appropriate for passive moving images only if they can be made sufficiently legible under the relevant conditions. In section C 5.3.1 "Blinking" we discuss the limits of the passive moving image in greater detail. <

/ C 5.3.1
LIMITS OF THE PASSING
MOVING IMAGE

B 3.4 / MANIPULATING DATA

In some cases, certain means are deliberately employed in order to manipulate data, but it is also possible to falsify the data in charts unknowingly with inappropriate design. In what follows we explain possibilities of conscious and unconscious manipulation of data in information graphics and the risks associated with it. >

/ FURTHER READING
An extensive discussion of the subject of graphic integrity can be found in EDWARD R. TUFTE'S *The Visual Display of Quantitative Information*.

B 3.4.1 / THE ZERO POINT

The zero point of a statistic diagram is indispensable to assessing developments correctly. It marks the baseline of the data and usually the viewer will assume its position out of habit. Hence its absence can lead to misinterpretations – an outcome that disreputable marketers sometimes intend. Depending on the surrounding layout or format, it may only be necessary to present a detail from the chart. Such a change should then be indicated. With a moving image, the problem of limited space for the depiction, which is what often leads to an axis being shortened or the zero point being left out of visual statistics, can be circumnavigated by means of an animation. It is possible, for example, to first present an overview of the relevant graphic and then zoom in on the corresponding detail to emphasize it. < The switch between the two views should be animated in order to illustrate the change in axes and zero point.

/ C 3
VOICE OVER
/ C 5
GUIDING THE
VIEWER'S ATTENTION

Changing the animated representation is only possible with a moving image.

B 3.4.2 / ALTERING QUANTITIES

Change in values should be illustrated one-dimensionally – e.g., using a bar chart. This permits more precise perception of the differences in comparison to area and volume charts. In such charts, the precise changes can usually be read only up to a point, so that the relationship between the values becomes very important. With extremely divergent values, it may become necessary to use an area chart, which enables one to present the value differences in two dimensions (rather than the single dimension of a bar chart). If one chooses to do so, it is essential that the comparative areas have, as much as possible, the same shape, differing only in size (ideally circles or squares). In a moving image, changes in scale can be illustrated by means of animations, making the process of growth more plausible. > **FIG. 6**

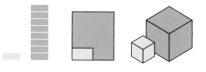

FIG. 6
Each of the three depictions shows the relationship correctly. Nevertheless, the one-dimensional change of the bar chart is the easiest one to interpret.

B 3.4.3 / PERSPECTIVE

Presentation tools, such as MICROSOFT POWERPOINT and APPLE KEYNOTE, often include numerous functions to produce visually striking 3-D charts. Generally, such forms of presentation are employed to grab the viewer's attention with the look of the graphic. Moreover, a classic diagram is always associated with expectations derived from school learning, which in some cases can cause the viewer to lose interest quickly. In that respect, the graphic presentation of information can become tightrope walking between aesthetic appearance and an accurate presentation of the underlying data; between entertaining and communicating information. The latter is and should be the goal of every information graphic. Designers have to ensure that the integrity of the content can withstand the visual effects necessary to ensure that the viewer "sticks it out." This also applies to the use of perspective in charts, which can often make the data more difficult to read. As long as perspective does not compromise what is supposed to be communicated, it can be considered a legitimate means of design. Its use is also dependent on the context of the graphic in question. The following principles should be observed: In an animated information graphic, movement in space makes 3-D representation possible under certain circumstances as well as a limited perspective (distortion). Only in 2-D representations will it result in extreme distortion, because three dimensions are reduced to two. Isometric rendering should be avoided in moving images because it does not correspond to a perspective familiar from experience and hence contradict the expected three-dimensionality of a moving image.

The viewer of an animated information graphic has only the predetermined time to take it in and also get a sense of its credibility. On a news broadcast, there is usually just enough time to grasp visually the graphic's core message as stated by the newscaster. It is usually not possible to question the data shown. The accuracy of the data thus ultimately depends on the designer's scrupulousness and sense of responsibility.

B 3.5 / REDUCTION

The role of graphic reduction for legibility in information graphics was already made evident above in the context of the CORE MESSAGE. In TUFTE's view, graphics often miss the real point because redundant design elements are employed. He analyzed a number of statistical graphics with this in mind, making a distinction between significant elements (data ink) and redundant components (nondata ink). "The larger the share of a graphic's ink devoted to the data, the better." < With this goal in mind, TUFTE demonstrated ways to reduce nondata ink. For example, in a bar chart, the line indicating the vertical axis can be left out without reducing legibility. > FIG. 7 And so, the graphic becomes clearer and hence is simpler for the viewer to interpret. Chartjunk, which already has been mentioned above, also belongs in the category of nondata ink. However, TUFTE primarily uses the term to refer to elements of a graphic employed more for the purpose of creative design than for any informational purpose. In TUFTE's view, the term chartjunk includes the use of patterns of all kinds, such as hatching or excessive use of grids in the background of a chart, and all elements that can be attributed solely to the designer's creative urge and that serve merely as decoration. <

An unimpeachable presentation of statistical data in a passive moving image should dispense with such decoration as much as possible, allowing the viewer to concentrate on the essential. As noted above, however, an overly reduced design can be perceived as off-putting or boring, depending on the target audience. The degree of reduction must therefore be chosen accordingly, without detracting from an understanding of the graphic in question.

/ EDWARD R. TUFTE:
*The Visual Display of
Quantitative Information,*
p. 92

/ EDWARD R. TUFTE:
*The Visual Display of
Quantitative Information,*
p. 107 – 121

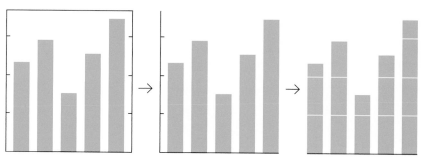

FIG. 7

B4 /
BASIC CONDITIONS OF THE MOVING IMAGE

A MOVING IMAGE LIMITS THE DEGREE OF COMPLEXITY THAT CAN BE DEPICTED.

Different rules apply to moving image and to print graphics. The main difference is that a moving image does not consist of a single image. Only the stringing together of several images creates a sequence and hence the illusion of movement for the viewer. This stringing together is called animation.

Several technical requirements must be observed when creating an animation. Just as there are different color profiles in print, the moving image has a number of possible settings that must be observed to obtain a high-quality result even after the rendering process. The following chapter provides an overview of these standards and explains the various formats that are significant for the moving image.

B 4.1 / FORMATS AND RESOLUTIONS

As with print media, it is necessary to determine the desired format for a moving picture (TV, internet, mobile devices, etc.) in advance and then base further work on that. One important difference from print, however, is that the moving image is a purely pixel-based medium. One consequence of this is that once a format has been chosen, it cannot be scaled to a larger size without considerable loss of quality, since enlargement requires that missing pixels be interpolated. Consequently, if there is still uncertainty about the actual distribution medium at the time a project is begun, it makes sense to begin with a format that is larger but has the same proportions.

Reducing the format also requires interpolation, but of a less drastic and more easily controllable sort, because the content is not supplemented but reduced. Nevertheless, problems with the thickness of lines and with type sizes can still occur, which result in a reduced legibility of the graphic.

A pixel, abbreviated px, is the smallest unit of a digital graphic. If we assume a pixel aspect ratio to be 1024 × 576, there are 589,824 pixels to be filled. The various media (Web players, mobile phone displays, monitors) have different pixel aspect ratios, but they all have a resolution of 72 DPI, however. That alone makes it clear that in comparison with print media, which is 300 DPI, the display area is extremely limited. Depicting a circle as roundly as possible takes up considerably much more space on a mobile phone display (320 × 240 px) than on a TXT-monitor with a resolution of 1440 × 900 px. There is no way to make the circle smaller on a mobile phone display because the pixel size is the same on both devices. > FIG. 1

Pixels are squares arranged in a grid and assigned specific information. This information contains values that define a certain color or brightness. The color model of a pixel differs from that of printing. Whereas the later uses the subtractive CMYK (Cyan, Magenta, Yellow, Black) color model, the moving image makes use of the additive RGB (Red, Green, Blue) color model.

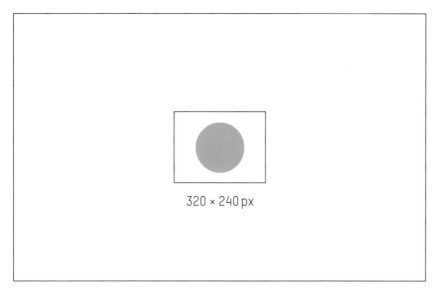

1440 × 900 px

320 × 240 px

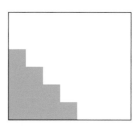

FIG. 1
Resolution of a mobile phone
display compared to a TFT display

Detail view of the circle's pixelated
border

The most common system is the RGB color model with eight bits per channel. A color depth of one bit would mean that precisely two states would be possible in each color channel. For example, for the red color channel they would be black and red. With a color depth of two bits, four states would be possible, namely, black, dark red, medium red, and bright red. In the case of the common color depth of eight bits, $2^8 = 256$ shades are available. Consequently, 3×8 bits $= 256 \times 256 \times 256 = 16,777,216$ different colors can be represented.

Individual pixels can also have an alpha channel that contains information about transparency.

The fixed size of a pixel has consequences for design. For example, a line cannot be depicted sharply if it is smaller than one pixel.

B 4.1.1 / PIXEL FORMATS

There are two principle possibilities for arranging pixels on a screen: as squares or hexagons. For example, the typical LCD monitor has a matrix of small crystals, with three subpixels in the primary colors red, green, and blue that are combined into a square pixel.

By contrast, the pixels of cathode ray tubes have a hexagonal arrangement, as can easily be seen by examining an older television with a magnifying glass.

The distortion *(long faces)* that sometimes occurs on self-produced video CDS results from the deliberate use of a false conversion rate of anamorphically encoded videos[1].

The following overview presents the various pixel aspect ratios for television and cinema.

---

1   Anamorphic widescreen videos are compressed in width but their height is unaltered.

B 4.1.2 / PICTURE FORMATS

TELEVISION

Traditional TV

720 × 576 px (corresponds to 414,720 pixels)

4:3 (1.33:1), 16:9 (1.78:1)

DVD

720 × 576 px (corresponds to 414,720 pixels)

HIGH DEFINITION (HD)

HDTV 720p (HD Ready) > 1280 × 720 px (corresponds to 921,600 pixels)

HDTV 1080i (Full HD) > 1920 × 1080 px (corresponds to 2,073,600 pixels)

CINEMA

Academy > 1.37:1

Cinema > 1.66:1

Cinema Wide > 1.85:1

CinemaScope > 2.35:1 or 2.39:1

B 4.1.3 / PAL SIGNAL (PHASE ALTERNATING LINE)

The PAL system is a color encoding system for analogue television. It was developed with the objective of automatically compensating for disturbing color errors, which with the NTSC system could only be balanced manually and inadequately. The basis for this system is the idea that two adjacent lines of an image will have more similarities than differences because images consist of planes. The PAL signal uses an image transfer rate of 25 frames per second. This is the rate at which a moving sequence begins to appear fluid to a viewer.

Movies are shot at 24 frames per second. As a result, PAL devices shorten the running time by 4 percent. This faster frame rate (PAL speedup) is scarcely perceived by humans. The sound reproduction is the only noticeable change. It is about a half-pitch higher, and some may notice a piece of music familiar from the original (or from CD) is being played back faster.

B 4.1.4 / NTSC-SIGNAL (NATIONAL TELEVISION SYSTEMS COMMITTEE)

The term NTSC derives from the eponymous American institution that established the first color broadcasting system for analogue television signals in many countries in the Americas and East Asia.

Unlike PAL, NTSC has 29.97 frames per second. The individual frames are composed of two half-images by writing an uneven and an even line in a field in alternation. This results in a nearly flicker-free image at 59.95 Hz. PAL and SECAM, both of which operate at 50 Hz, are more susceptible to flickering.[2]

B 4.1.5 / SECAM SIGNAL *(SÉQUENTIEL COULEUR À MÉMOIRE)*

This analogue television standard is employed primarily in France and Eastern Europe. Its objective was to improve color reproduction relative to NTSC with less than ideal reception. SECAM uses frequency modulation rather than the amplitude modulation of PAL and NTSC. It uses YDdDr[3] color, which, much like the better-known YUV[4], consists of a brightness signal (Y) and two color difference signals (Db and Dr). The image repetition rate is 50 Hz.

B 4.1.6 / ACTION-SAFE AND TITLE-SAFE

Another very important point when designing moving images is observing the action safe area and the title safe area. This is a safe area within the film image. Remaining within this area ensures no information will be lost. Common editing and animation software offers the option of showing these areas and choosing between 4:3 and 16:9 displays. The action safe area is 5 percent smaller than the total image; the title safe area is 10 percent smaller.

As a general guideline, it can be assumed that the safe area is 10 percent for old CRT televisions and ca. 2–5 percent for TFT displays. For an animated information graphic, this means that all the significant elements must lie within the title safe area. > FIG. 3

The double-page spread that follows offers an overview of the above-mentioned formats. > FIGS. 4 & 5

FIG. 2
Wordwide allocation of the NTSC-,
PAL- and Secam-signals

FIG. 3
Title-safe, Action-safe

---

2   The difference in display refresh rates between NTSC and the two other video formats, PAL and SECAM, is the biggest problem when converting a video. Whereas with PAL the film can simply be played back 4 percent faster, with NTSC (at ca. 30 frames per second) the film has to be played back about 25 percent faster without changing the frame rate. Instead, four frames are extended to five frames by means of so-called interlacing.

3   YDbDr employs three components to represent image information: luminance Y (also *luma*, brightness per area) and two chrominance components (color components): Db and Dr. Hence, it should be categorized as a luminance/chrominance color model.

4   YUV employs two components to represent image information: luminance Y (also *luma*, brightness per area) and chrominance (also *chroma*, the color component), with the latter composed of two subcomponents U and V.

PAL

Secam

NTSC

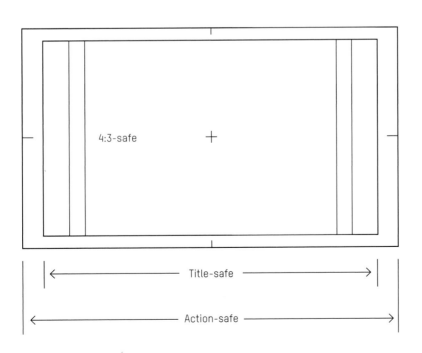

FIG. 4

/ PIXEL ASPECT RATIO (PAR)

A mathematical ratio that describes
how the width of a pixel in a digital
image compares to the height of that
pixel.

HD 1080i

HD 720p / youtube.com (HD / 16:9) / vimeo.com (HD)

FIG. 5

Relationships between various
ratios

4:3

1.33:1   1.66:1   1.85:1   2.35:1

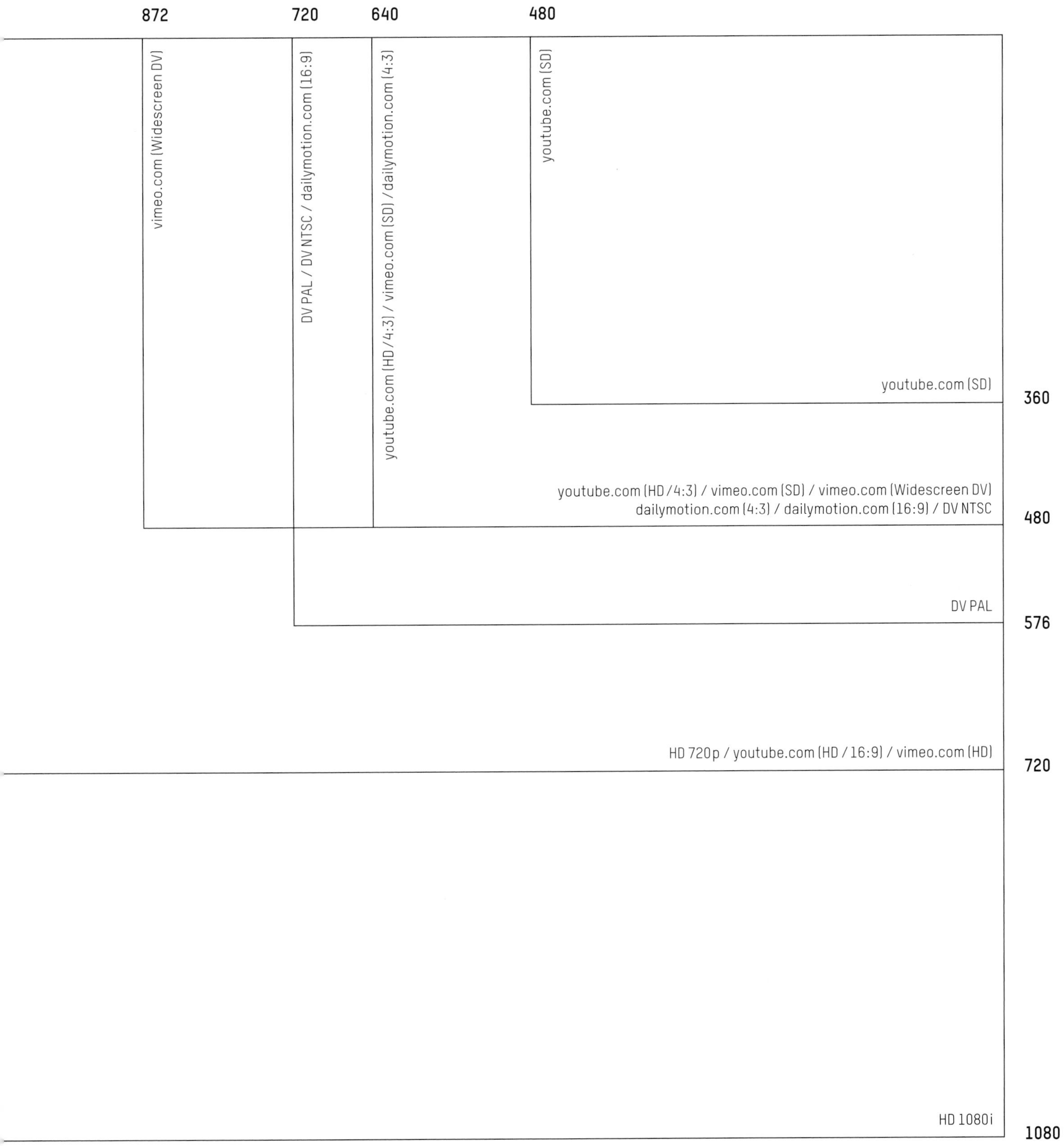

872	720	640	480		

vimeo.com (Widescreen DV)

DV PAL / DV NTSC / dailymotion.com (16:9)

youtube.com (HD / 4:3) / vimeo.com (SD) / dailymotion.com (4:3)

youtube.com (SD)

youtube.com (SD) — 360

youtube.com (HD / 4:3) / vimeo.com (SD) / vimeo.com (Widescreen DV)
dailymotion.com (4:3) / dailymotion.com (16:9) / DV NTSC — 480

DV PAL — 576

HD 720p / youtube.com (HD / 16:9) / vimeo.com (HD) — 720

HD 1080i — 1080

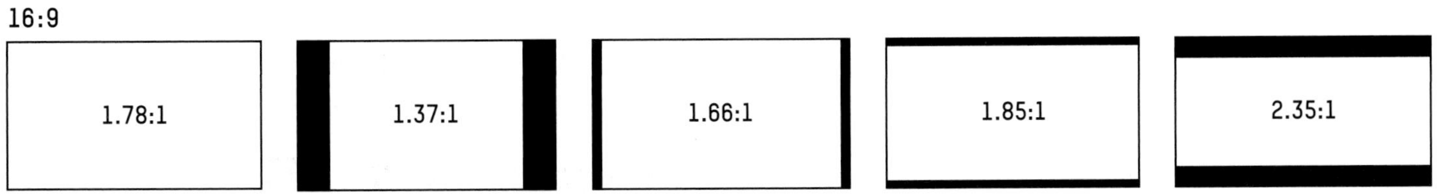

16:9

1.78:1	1.37:1	1.66:1	1.85:1	2.35:1

B 4.2 / TYPOGRAPHY

In animations and moving images in general, the perception of typography differs from that of print media. It depends on several factors, including type size, typeface, the speed of the animation, and the length of time the typography can be seen. In moving images, san serif typefaces contribute to legibility. This is because serifs can run together, making type more difficult to read at small type sizes, low resolution, or when compressed.

/ "On screen […] sans serif types are more suitable, because the delicate series cannot be displayed well at low screen resolutions […] Only larger than a certain size (depending on the typeface, 16 points and upward) can serif typefaces be displayed unproblematically." <

/ FRANK THISSEN:
Screen-, Design-, Handbuch,
p. 93

It appears to be difficult to provide universal values for type sizes. They depend on the distribution medium, on the one hand, and on the typeface used, on the other. As a general guideline, with a resolution of 1024 × 576 pixels, one can recommend a typeface of at least 16 pixels.

It is also advisable to increase letter spacing to improve the legibility of type. This also keeps the letters from running together. Attention should also be paid to having sufficient leading to avoid interference between lines.

A: Easy Ease In   B: Easy Ease   C: Easy Ease Out   D: Normal

Opacity 0–100 %
in 1 sec.

	A INFORMOTION B INFORMOTION C INFORMOTION D INFORMOTION	A INFORMOTION B INFORMOTION C INFORMOTION D INFORMOTION

Opacity 100–0 %
in 1 sec.

A INFORMOTION B INFORMOTION C INFORMOTION D INFORMOTION	A INFORMOTION B INFORMOTION C INFORMOTION D INFORMOTION	A INFORMOTION B INFORMOTION C INFORMOTION D INFORMOTION

0 fps   5   10

Contrary to TUFTE's view that typography with borders is confusing and consti-
tutes unnecessary junk, it can indeed make sense in a moving image, since type has
to be placed on a moving background. This avoids flickering type, and if the proper
color is chosen for the background, it provides sufficient contrast for reading.

The length of time a text is visible is also crucial to legibility. Designers should
keep in mind that short words can be read more quickly than long ones. In their
book *Raster für das Bewegtbild*, TANJA DIEZMANN and TOBIAS GREMMLER offer
the guideline of one second per syllable. ‹ This also pertains to the length of words
in headings.

Finally, it must be decided whether the text is simply faded in or animated. In the
latter case, keep in mind that animation shortens the time during which the text
is legible. Software such as Adobe After Effects offers Easy Ease technology to
increase the amount of time. The time for fading in and out can be shortened while
still obtaining the desired effect, giving the viewer more time to read. ‹ (see below)
As the example shows, Easy Ease In is suited for fading in and Easy Ease Out for
fading out. This maximizes the time when the typography is 100 percent opaque
and most visible.

/ TANJA DIEZMANN,
TOBIAS GREMMLER:
Raster für das Bewegtbild,
p. 22

/ TANJA DIEZMANN,
TOBIAS GREMMLER:
Raster für das Bewegtbild,
p. 23

A INFORMOTION	A INFORMOTION	A INFORMOTION
B INFORMOTION	B INFORMOTION	B INFORMOTION
C INFORMOTION	C INFORMOTION	C INFORMOTION
D INFORMOTION	D INFORMOTION	D INFORMOTION

A INFORMOTION		
B INFORMOTION	B INFORMOTION	
C INFORMOTION	C INFORMOTION	
D INFORMOTION	D INFORMOTION	

15   20   25

B 4.3 / THE LIMITS OF THE PASSIVE MOVING IMAGE

As explained in the two previous sections, the design of moving images has been influenced by changes in circumstances. On the one hand, the decrease in resolution relative to print media limits the design in terms of size and richness of detail. On the other hand, the sequential and time-dependent nature of the medium has consequences. According to BERTIN, changes in the process of perception play an important role:

/ "An incursion into cinematographic expression very quickly reveals that most of its laws are substantially different from the laws of atemporal drawing. Although movement introduces only one additional variable, it is an overwhelming one; it so dominates perception that it severely limits the attention which can be given to the meaning of the other variables." <

/ JACQUES BERTIN:
Semiology of Graphics,
p. 42

What effects do these facts have on the creation of information graphics as passive moving images?

B 4.3.1 / REDUCED COMPLEXITY

The primary effect of the two factors just mentioned, resolution and time, is the complexity of representation that is possible. Lower resolution limits the number of details that can be depicted. Time plays an even larger role in this context, since it sets clear limits on the time available for the viewer to perceive individual elements.

TUFTE has defended highly complex data sets as the basis for a visualization. In his view, good visual statistics and maps must make as much information possible available in as little space as possible, and hence they have high density of data. In contrast to a static graphic in which the data density is processed in a single image, it has to be distributed within a series of images in a moving image. > **FIG. 4**

As a consequence, perception – and hence the data density that can be conveyed – is considerably reduced by the available time.

FIG. 4
In a moving image, data density is distributed throughout the available time.

This can tax the viewer's attention.

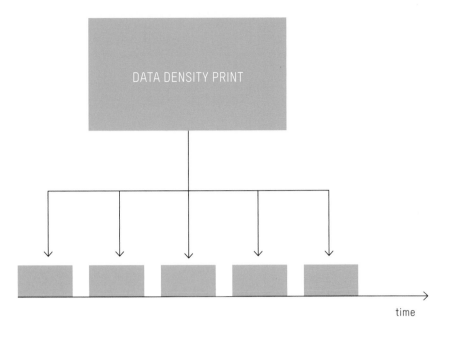

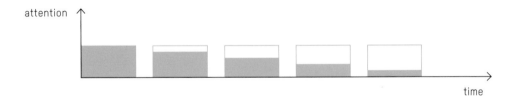

B 4.3.2 / LIMITED DESIGN OPTIONS

The moving image, like every other medium, has design limitations that result from resolution. Delicate structures of lines or patterns are limited by the actual size of a pixel. The hairlines and fine grids that are frequently used in print media cannot be reproduced here and result in undesirable moiré patterns[5] in moving images.

As described in chapter B 4.2 "Typography," there are also strict limits on typography. < Moreover, all the design means employed in information graphics have to be considered in terms of the whether they can be perceived within the available time. For example, it might be necessary to reduce the significant shades of a color from ten to five. <

/ B 4.2
TYPOGRAPHY

/ C 2.1.3
TYPOGRAPHY
/ B 5
STORYBOARD

---

5   Moiré patterns occur when grids or lines overlap.

B 4.3.3 / LINEARITY

In defining the term passive moving image, we established that it does not offer the viewer any opportunity for interaction. Consequently, the structure of the content of an animated information graphic is linear. Hence the narrative sequence has a fixed time. In contrast to print media and interactive applications, the viewer's perception is focused on a series of preselected facts.

B 4.3.4 / ATTENTION

Like the director of a movie, the designer of animated information graphics needs to be sure that the viewers do not "walk out." It is not enough simply to point out the details one after the other.

There has to be a well-thought-out narrative concept to entertain the viewers and keep them interested for the duration of the animation.

/ C1
NARRATION
/ B5
STORYBOARD

The concept has to be planned and drawn up at the beginning of every project. An engaging design appropriate to its target audience is equally as important. A simplified scientific presentation in the manner of TUFTE and BERTIN is appropriate only for animations intended for specialist audiences. For example, when the operation of the eye is explained to a tenth grade biology class, the graphic has to be adjusted in terms of both design and tempo. Students have viewing habits that differ from those of the attendees of a scientific conference.

If the designer wants to hold the viewer's attention for a long time, he or she has to walk a tightrope between a presentation appropriate to the context and communicating the intended information.

Animated information graphics as passive moving images have many advantages and design possibilities, as well as various limitations. It is important to consider whether a given data set or state of affairs can be presented suitably.

ANIMATED INFOGRAPHICS

HAVE MANY ADVANTAGES AND DESIGN POSSIBILITIES AS WELL AS VARIOUS LIMITATIONS.

B5 /
STORYBOARD

THE STORYBOARD STRUCTURES ALL OF THE STEPS IN A PROCESS TO AVOID UNNECESSARY EFFORT.

Creating a storyboard is a very important step when producing an animated information graphic. Especially when larger teams are collaborating, it can help avoid unnecessary difficulties to come to an agreement and give all the participants a clear idea of what the intended result is.

In general, *storyboarding* refers to a way of organizing and listing the graphic elements or illustrations – that is, it is graphic equivalent of a screenplay drawn by hand or on the computer.

The technique for writing storyboard was developed in the early 1930s by Walt Disney Studios. Over time the technique has been used not only in animated films but increasingly in feature films, having become an essential part of the production process.

The storyboard visualizes the scenes as they will appear through the camera. It primarily serves the director – or, in the case of animated information graphics, the concept designer – as a way of translating the storyline that has been developed into concrete images. Because the effort to produce it can be considerable, especially in the case of animations. It is essential to agree on many steps – such as tracking shots, framing, transitions, and cuts – as early as possible in order to minimize the animation necessary later. Possible problems can thus be resolved early on. This can reduce unnecessary work in subsequent steps, and all the team members (customer, copywriter, graphic designer, motion designer) get a clear idea what the film should look like.

The storyboard also offers an overview of the entire story and all the key features available in the relevant resources.

In addition to visuals, technical details and the use of voice over and sound can also be indicated. In this stage, the storyboard artist can consider strategies and techniques to reduce the visual complexity by using voice over and sound and thus improve the reception of information.

/ C 3
VOICE OVER
/ C 4
SOUND

STORYBOARD-SAMPLE

FRAME	SHOT	TEXT	CONTENT	TIME
24	SPECIALTY DRUG		But benefits suffer from industryrelatedcosts,too.	00:56
25		As cost of treatments with these specialty...		00:56
26		... drug spendings increased.		00:56
42	CLINICAL DECISION SUPPORT / DID YOU TRY THS	with intelligent algorithms that support	and treatment schedule	01:32
43	DID YOU TRY THS / 90% / 20$ DISCOUNT	clinical decision-making		01:32
44	90% / 20$ / YES / NO			01:32

Stefan Fichtel,
ixtract GmbH

FRAME	SHOT	TEXT	CONTENT	TIME
47				01:42
48		Let's make it easy for doctors to explain the choices and collaborate with patients		01:42
49			Visualization of provider selection (Google Maps)	01:42

FINAL SCENES

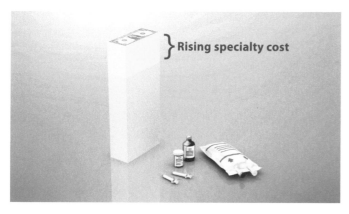

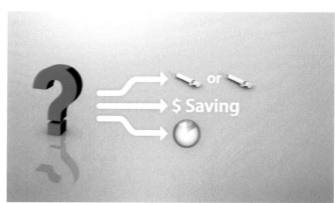

Frame 26 & 43

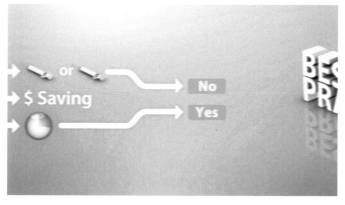

Frame 44 & 49

135

B 5.1 / ANIMATICS

Once the storyboard has been completed, it is realized as an animatic. An animatic is a filmed storyboard. The individual scenes are edited together and perhaps roughly animated to give a better sense of motion and timing. The simplest form of an animatic is a sequence of stills from the storyboard. Whenever possible, the soundtrack or voice over is already added. To get a sense of the speed of the spoken text, it is advisable to have the voice over read during the draft phase. At that point, it will quickly become evident whether the sound and images are coordinated and whether the timing of all the transitions is right.

If corrections are necessary, the storyboard is changed accordingly. Only then should the animation process begin. As soon as all the specialists are working on it, changes are not just expensive but also much more complicated in terms of coming to agreements and organizing time.

The animatic can be animated with small zooms or tracking shots to simulate the movement of a camera.

B 5.2 / WORKFLOW OVERVIEW

There are five big challenges to create a proper information graphic:

1 / Researching the subject adequately.

2 / Adressing the target audience.

3 / Deciding what key messages will be communicated.

4 / Finding the appropriate form of presentation.

5 / Considering the medium and the restrictions or possibilities it implies.

WORKFLOW

DATASET

COMMUNICATION METHOD		
STATIC	MOTION	INTERACTIVE
Information presented in its entirely at one glance	Informationpresentedprogressively in a linear sequence	Information presented selectively based on viewer's choice
Newspapergraphics, mapfolders, productmauals, expository diagrams	Animation or graphic overlays on live action video	Usually Web-based information units which are narrative, instructive, simulative, or explorative in nature

INFOGRAPHIC DEVICE		
DIAGRAMS	MAPS	CHARTS
ICON / Show visually simplified reality	**LOCATOR** / Show location of something in relation to something else	**FLOW** / Show magnitude changes over time
SEQUENCE / Show succession of events, actions, and casual relationships	**DATA** / Show quantitative information in relation to its geographic location	**BAR** / Show proportionate comparisons of magnitude
PROCESS / Show step-by-step interactionsacrossbothspace and time	**SCHEMATIC** / Show abstracted representation of geography, process, or sequence	**PIE** / Show distribution of parts of a whole
TIMELINE / Show chronological progression		**ORGANIZATION** / Show parts in a structureandtheirrelationship with each other
EXPOSITION / Show details or points of view normally not available to the human eye suchascutaways, axonometric views, etc.		

INFORMATION TYPE		
SPATIAL	CHRONOLOGICAL	QUANTITATIVE
Information that describes relative positions and spatial relationships in a physical or conceptual location	Information that describes sequentialpositionsandcausal relationships in a physical or conceptual timeline	Information that describes scale, proportion, change, and organization of quantities in space, time, or both

INFOGRAPHIC

> online content available
(please find a unique code
at the end of this book)

MEANS OF IMPLEMENTATION

C1/
NARRATION

VIEWERS ARE POINTED TOWARDS CERTAIN DETAILS OF A SITUATION WITHIN A PREDETER-MINED TEMPORAL SEQUENCE.

Unlike print graphics or interactive Web applications, the information graphic in a passive moving image is always tied to a linear sequence that is subject to temporal restrictions. That is to say, the viewer is pointed toward certain details of a state of affairs in a fixed temporal sequence.

As with a traditional film, the viewer of an animated information graphic follows a given plotline.

And like the director of a film, the designer of an animated information graphic has to ensure that the viewer's attention is held for the full length of the sequence. The narration provides an appealing dramaturgy and an arc of tension necessary to achieve this.

C 1.1 / MINIMAL STRUCTURE

Narration is the temporal and spatial organization of a narrated plot in a sequence. It is defined by a beginning and end or by an initial situation and the transformation of at least one feature that brings about a final situation (minimal structure). This structure can be summed up as follows: <

/ COLIN WARE
Visual Thinking: for Design,
p. 138

/ **Presentation of the problem**
/ **Coming up with the solution**
/ **Solution**

Applied to the example of the instruction for assembling a table, the following steps result:

/ **Presentation of the problem** / The parts of a table are to be assembled
/ **Coming up with the solution** / How the parts relate to one another and assembly of the parts
/ **Solution** / The assembled table

see **FIG. 1**

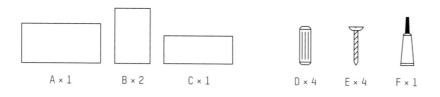

A × 1   B × 2   C × 1   D × 4   E × 4   F × 1

Presentation of the problem

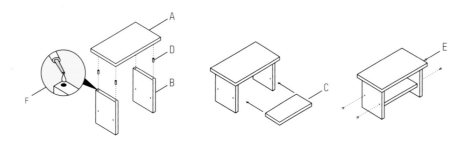

Coming up with the solution

Solution

FIG. 1
Minimal Structure

From a didactic perspective, the content of an information graphic should be reduced to one main message and a few secondary messages. < Once this step has been made, the designer has to arrange the messages in a logical narrative sequence in accordance with the structure described here. With more complicated situations in particular, producing a storyboard can be a great help or even an absolute necessity to achieve this. <

/ ANGELA JANSEN
Handbuch der Infografik,
p. 88

/ B 4
STORYBOARD

C 1.1.1 / MEANS OF IMPLEMENTATION

The term *narration* describes not only the narrative structure, but also how it is implemented. In the context of animated information graphics, this includes the visual means of the graphic and image on the one hand, and the audio means of voice over and sound on the other. <

/ C 3
VOICE OVER
/ C 4
SOUND

In the moving image, information can be transmitted through two channels: the visual channel and the audio channel.

In addition, elements of cinematic narration such as *editing* and *camera angles* can also be employed.

/ "Moving the viewpoint in a visualization can function as a form of narrative control. Often a virtual camera is moved from one part of a data space to another, drawing attention to different features." <

/ COLIN WARE
Information Visualization:
Perception for Design,
p. 327

It should be noted, however, that not all these techniques are suitable for use in information graphics. In contrast to film, which leaves the viewer partially in the dark to create tension or confused by rapid cuts, the goals of an information graphic is to communicate information quickly, clearly, and unequivocally. In the sections that follow we examine the possibilities for using editing and camera angles.

C 1.2 / EDITING

Nearly every film and every animation consists of individual sequences of images that describe different aspects of a state of affairs. They are assembled into an overall composition by means of editing. Every single shot[1] contains aspects of so-called mise-en-scène. The latter term describes, on the one hand, the staging of a scene with sets, costumes, and decorations and, on the other, cinematic components such as the composition of the image and the tracking shots. With the aid of editing, connections between the individual shots are created, producing effects of continuity or of contrasts.

The effect of continuity is very important when creating animated information graphics. The editing has to be attentive to the information that the graphic is to communicate; it should guide the viewer and minimize the latitude for interpretation.

---

1 The term *shot* refers to a series of individual images recorded by a film camera without interruption. The individual shots are later edited to make the complete film.

C 1.2.1 / CONTINUITY

The term *continuity* describes the transition between shots in terms of its effect on the viewer. The viewing habits and expectations of the latter play a role as well. WARE illustrates this with an example:

/ "If a car travels out of one side of the frame in one scene, it should arrive in the next scene travel-
ing in the same direction (for example, from left to right); otherwise the audience may lose track
of it and pay attention to something else." < > **FIG. 2**

/ COLIN WARE
*Information Visualization:
Perception for Design*,
p. 328

Keeping to this principle will avoid perplexing the viewers and hold their attention. WARE mentions this in the context of so-called anchors, which help the viewer establish the relationships between different scenes:

/ "Certain visual objects may act as visual reference points, or anchors, tying one view of a data
space to the next. [...] When cuts are made from one view to another, ideally, several anchors
should be visible from the previous frame." <

/ COLIN WARE
*Information Visualization:
Perception for Design*,
p. 328

C 1.2.2 / SPLIT SCREEN

In a split screen, the existing display area is divided into one or more zones in order to depict several actions simultaneously. This technique is used, for example, in the American television series *24* in order to viewer simultaneous actions by different protagonists in parallel.

Hence this technique is suited to illustrate parallel processes and their connections. Because the human eye can only focus on one point at any given time, it is essential to keep in mind that all of the processes should not be animated at the same time. The brain is able to register several points in the visual field at the same time, but they are not perceived fully.

Consequently, the simultaneous depiction of corresponding processes should not be confused with their simultaneous occurrence. Here, too, one has to follow a narrative sequence and thus only emphasize one part of the screen at any given time. There are several possibilities open to designers to guide the viewer's attention to focus on the corresponding area. < > **FIG. 3**

/ C5
FOCUSING THE
VIEWER'S ATTENTION

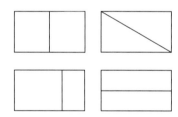

Split screen:
here with two segments each.

FIG. 3
In these examples, the transition
is shown in split screen in order
to present the dialogue between
the people concerned and their
surroundings.

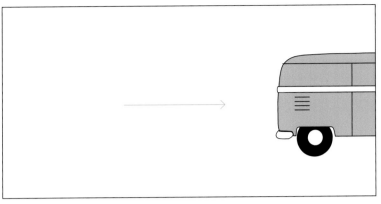
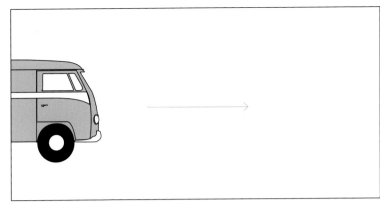

FIG. 2

shot 1

shot 2

FIG. 3A

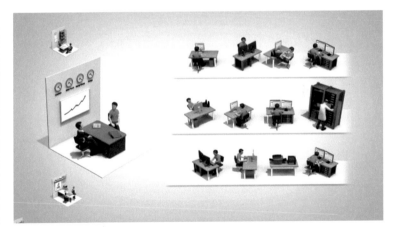

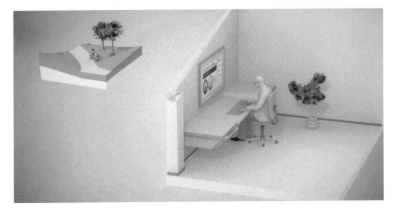

FIG. 3B

C 1.2.3 / CONTINUITY EDITING (CLASSICAL NARRATION)

As the name already indicates, continuity editing is a form of montage that works as subtly as possible. The viewer is supposed to concentrate solely on the events, and the absorption of information is not disturbed by abrupt cuts or rapid alternation between cuts.

Hence, the focus is on the information to be conveyed. In order to be as discreet as possible, the aforementioned principles of continuity should be respected. One scene should lead the viewer into the next scene. Then he or she will pay less attention to the cut. > **FIG. 4**

The individual sequences in this process open with a so-called *establishing shot*[2], which is intended to give the viewer an overview of the scene shown.

C 1.2.4 / LONG TAKE

In contrast to continuity editing, a long take dispenses with cuts entirely. It is often used in animated information graphics to depict processes e.g., illustrating a water treatment plant. The use of the camera plays an important role here. It helps keep the viewer focused on the separation stages. Following the principle of continuity, this kind of shot is well suited to conveying information.

C 1.2.5 / ZOOM

A zoom helps the viewer to follow visually a shift in the depiction – from an overall view to a detailed view, for example – while remained focused on what is shown. Elements of the graphic that are not significant at this point are removed from the viewer's visual field. Sometimes a close-up – that is, an abrupt cut from overview to detail – is used rather than a zoom. The zoom is always preferable in an animated information graphic, since an animated shift in presentation precludes from the outset the confusion that can potentially result from a cut. > **FIG. 5**

Other means of cinematic narration, such as the match cut,[3] are out of the question in the context of animated information graphics, since they deliberately confuse the viewer in order to produce cinematic tension.

FIG. 4
If an airplane disappears on the right side of the screen and flies in again from the left side, it maintains the natural movement.

FIG. 5
The converging arrows indicate the place where the camera will zoom. The circle clearly marks the area of the zoom.

2   The establishing shot describes the first shot of a sequence. It establishes the site of the action. Hence it provides the viewer with spatial and temporal orientation within the space of action.

3   Match cut describes an editing technique in which a movement is edited in, with the movement continuing in a subsequent scene. They are often spatially and temporally separate actions that appear to be connected as a result. The resulting continuity produces connections where none existed.

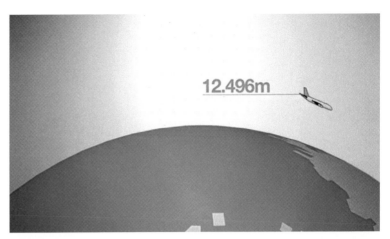

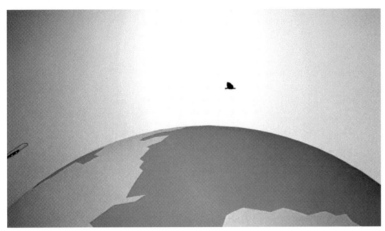

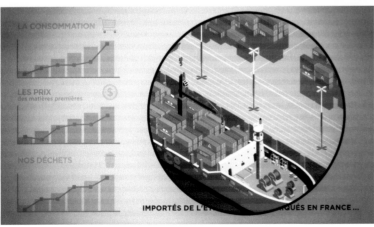

Animated information graphics must entertain.

Narrative means can help produce appealing, easily understood graphics. This is the only way to arouse long-term interest and retain attention. Employing an engaging rhythm brings one even closer to this goal.

C 1.2.6 / RHYTHM

The term "rhythm" describes the length of the individual shots in a sequence and their relationship to one another. In the case of an animated information graphic, the length of the individual shots also determines the time available for the user to absorb the information.

The concept of rhythm also refers to the animation of individual elements within a shot and the resulting visual dynamic. Do they move slowly or quickly, and how do they relate to one another?

Finally, in an animation it is also important that repeating elements appear similarly. For example, one should choose one way for the typography to blend in and then stick to it. It is confusing if it first fades in and then slides in. Moreover, the animation time should remain constant. Observing such regularity will help create a balanced animation.

In general, it should be said that every animated information graphic is in all respects a system with its own rules, which should be consciously established and then rigorously heeded for its duration. This helps the viewer to understand and follow the animation and to concentrate completely on the content being conveyed.

C 1.2.7 / TEMPO

Relating the individual shots rhythmically can also help to make the process of explaining more lively by varying the pace, thereby holding the viewer's attention without neglecting information. In schematic depictions, individual processes can be repeated. Here the designer has the opportunity to vary the tempo by depicting a process clearly so that the viewer will understand how it functions and then showing subsequent identical processes sped up. Slowing the tempo can also emphasize a particular point in the narration. < > FIG. 6

/ C1
NARRATION

Designers of moving images have to be able to combine individual images and information in a way that results in a logical connection and a narrative structure. In that process, the available narrative means have to be chosen carefully, since

/ B2.5
REDUCTION

the reduction everyone is seeking applies here as well. < All the means employed should serve rapid communication of the information and not be used for their own sake. Accomplished interplay of different components is the route to conveying all the important information while holding the viewer's attention.

FIG. 6
The first seconds of the scene show the detailed assembly of cars. As soon as the principle is clear, the tempo is increased, and the rest of the assembly can be shown with time-lapse photography.

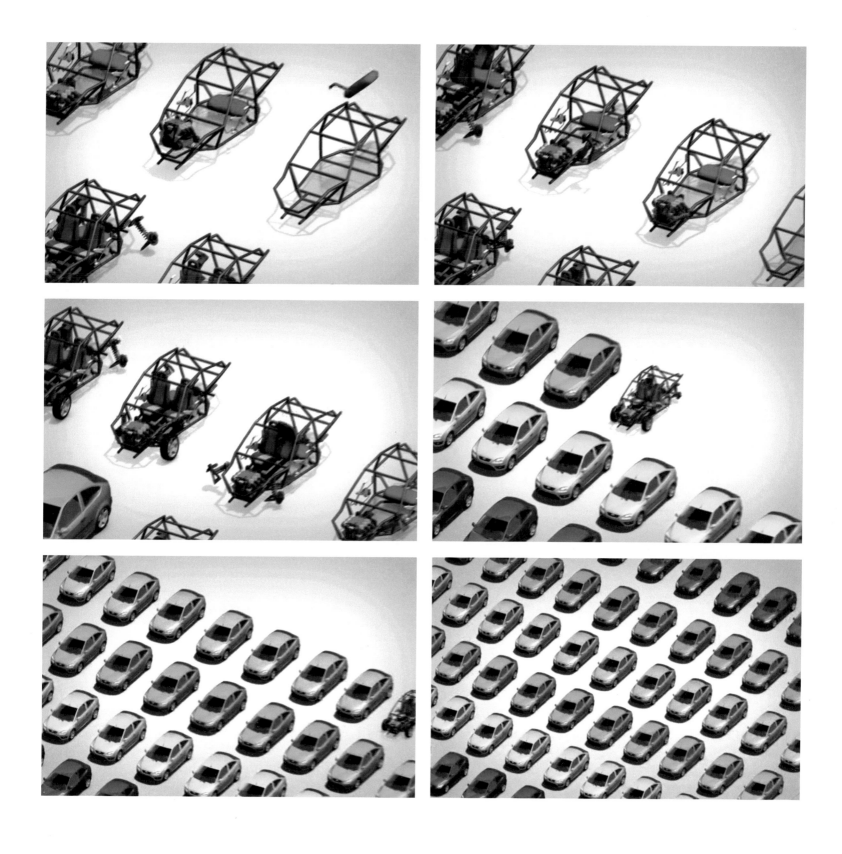

C 1.3 / CAMERA ANGLES

The use of information graphics in moving images offers an opportunity to employ different camera angles to observe an object or state of affairs from different points of view. The camera becomes the viewer's eye and focuses attention in a predetermined sequence on the relevant components or sections of the graphic.

The use of 3-D programs offers the designer of broad spectrum of options for representation. This diversity does not, however, necessarily add to the quality of the content. As with the use of editing, camera angles should primarily be chose to contribute to better understanding. The pages that follow explain the camera angles that can help a designer do justice to this task.

C 1.3.1 / VIEW FROM BELOW

The view from below (also called a low-angle shot) refers to a camera standpoint in which objects are recorded from a low vertical position.

This camera angle is often used to increase the size or height of an object. In film, this can trigger respect for the object in the viewer – a shot of the palace of an ominous ruler, for example. The so-called worm's-eye view is an extreme view from below. Low-angle shots are primarily dramaturgical in function. > FIG. 7

In animated information graphics, the use of low-angle shots can lead to distortion of the real object and hence of the underlying information or relationships. At times, however, positioning the camera in the lower part of the visual field can also be necessary to describe an object or its function precisely in a schematic drawing. The resulting distortion should be minimized and the visual axes kept largely perpendicular. The camera should therefore be kept as level as possible.

It is also possible to combine various camera angles if it helps convey information. For example, it is possible to imagine a view from above that introduces the surroundings. Then the camera switches to a view from below where the significant element is found and can then be explained.

C 1.3.2 / NORMAL VIEW

"In a normal view, the camera is at the same height as the object being filmed; in the case of an actor, this usually means at eye level." <

Normal view places the camera at the height of the object being filmed. The camera attempts to imitate natural perspective. A normal view can, however, also be considered a view from below or above. For example, in order to show a high-rise at full size from a perpendicular perspective, the camera has to be elevated. > FIG. 8

*de.wikipedia.org/wiki/
Kameraperspektive*

FIG. 7
Here the camera position is at the lower end of the wheel. Because the camera angle is horizontal, there is very little distortion.

FIG. 8
The camera position is at the same height as the significant elements.

C 1.3.3 / VIEW FROM ABOVE

An elevated vertical camera perspective looking down at the object is called a view from above (or high-angle shot). > **FIG. 9**

A view from above can be employed to give the viewer of a graphic an overall view on a spatially based principle. A bird's-eye view is an extreme form of the view from above in which the camera is at a right angle to the object and looks down at it. City maps are a common example of this. > **FIG. 10**

As mentioned in the context of cognitive form, animated information graphics should provide the viewer with an opportunity to grasp the object described as effortlessly as possible. < A suitable camera angle can assist in that process. Hence the designer should choose one accordingly.

/ C2.3.1
COGNITIVE FORM

It is always up to the designer to choose the correct perspective in relation to what needs to be communicated. As described at the beginning of the chapter, the technical possibilities for representation should not be misused.

During tracking shots, significant elements must remain in focus and should not cover other significant elements.

FIG. 9
View from above

FIG. 10
Bird's-eye view

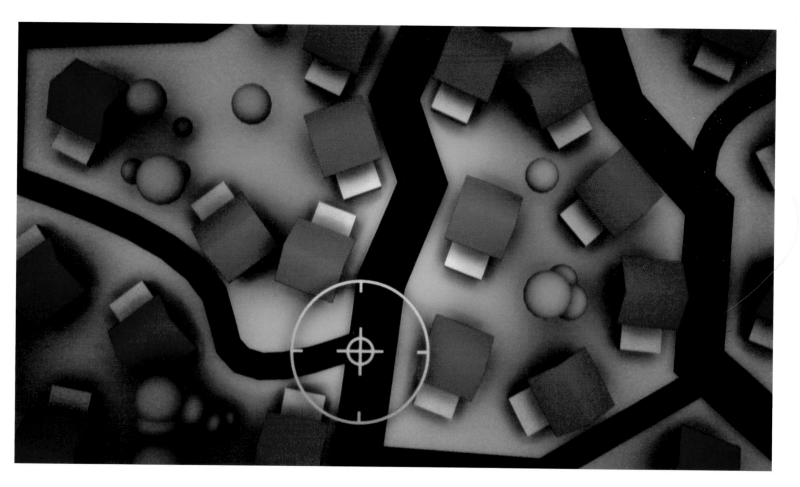

C2/
ANIMATION

ANIMATION CAN BE
USED TO CHANGE THE
VALUES OR STATES
OF OBJECTS IN A
TEMPORAL SEQUENCE.

Compared to static images, animations can depict changes, values, and states of objects more clearly. In some cases they are the only way to make these changes comprehensible. That is precisely what makes animated content so useful for information graphics.

Animation can show different states over time.

Changes over time can be illustrated continuously. The animation makes it possible to visualize changes in content or space. For example, forms can vary in size and appearance; colors in value; or objects in position. It is important to decide whether these changes are employed as significant elements themselves or serve rather to emphasize significant elements – to direct the viewer's gaze to a certain area of a graphic, for instance. In addition, animation offers the possibility of illustrating causal connections, thus revealing mutual dependencies between data, objects, and processes.

C 2.1 / COLOR

Above all, color exercises an undeniable psychological attraction. [...]
It captures and holds attention, multiplies the number of readers, assures better retention of the information, and, in short, increases the scope of the message. <

/ JACQUES BERTIN:
Semiology of Graphics,
p. 91

Information designers take advantage of this, when labeling or distinguishing individual elements and illustration or imitating real states. Although color also makes graphics generally livelier, one must be aware of its effect and potential meaning. This chapter begins by looking at the effect and significance of colors in contrast to other design elements. It explains how to select colors suited to information design and how to employ them specifically as a means to design an animated information graphic.

C 2.1.1 / COLOR DOMINANCE

Color is one of several ways to encourage the selective perception of an element or group of elements. If it is properly employed, you can guarantee getting of having the viewer's attention. Differentiating various subsections or levels of meaning in an information graphic plays an important role here. It is particularly important with an animation that the viewer not lose sight of the significant elements, since there is a risk that important information will be lost and the graphic will not be understood.

Color dominates form.

FIG. 1 shows a collection of blue and pink circles and squares. The image also has two blue squares that are initially harder to see. Only upon closer inspection do we see the blue squares, thus making it clear that the role of color dominates that of form.

The use of saturated colors is advisable to that end. The dominance of color is maximized near a saturated color and reduced as one moves away from its saturation point. The three primary colors – red, yellow, and blue – and the secondary colors, which consist of equal mixtures of the primary colors, are considered very clear colors. Colors of these values are thus particularly well suited for emphasizing things in a graphic. Differences in a color's temperature should also be considered. For example, if they appear together, cold colors (such as blue) recede more into the background than warm ones (such as red).

In this context, it should also be noted that juxtaposing of colors of equal brightness or value can result in undesirable flickering. The right contrast is crucial here.

C 2.1.2 / CLEAR CONTRASTS

A graphic should be constructed in such a way that the foreground can always be separated from the background. This is achieved by giving the background a desaturated, muted color and the elements conveying information a saturated, bright color. > FIG. 2

It becomes problematic when small color elements are used on a color background: all elements must be very clearly distinguishable – both from the background and from one another. In general: "The smaller the mark, the less distinguishable are the colors." < To prevent the colors of small elements from merging, there has to be sufficient contrast in brightness. The colors red, green, blue, and yellow offer the best contrast. For larger graphic elements, the contrasts need not be as extreme.

/ JACQUES BERTIN
Semiology of Graphics,
p. 89

FIG. 1
Even though their forms differ –
a circle in one case, a square in
another – the color indicates the
elements belong together.

FIG. 2
The significant element – in this
case, an Atlantic oil rig – stands
out against the monochromatic
background. The choice of color
for the typography is also based
on clear and strong contrasts.

294 ft

Strong contrasts are also necessary when important elements need to be emphasized with color.

The choice of color depends on the color of the object to be emphasized. When creating an animation, a suitable color for the entire sequence must be chosen.

To make typography more visible, for example, it is important to choose the correct contrast between the color of the background and of the type, or to place a surface behind the type to ensure that it is consistently legible. <

/ C5.1.2
FOCUSING THE
VIEWER'S ATTENTION

C 2.1.3 / COLOR AND REALITY

Color can depict our surroundings, place information in a familiar context, or enable us to categorize things within the whole more quickly.

Naturally, it is important to study in advance the correct choice of color and the psychological effects of color in advance, otherwise misunderstandings can easily arise. For example, mailboxes in Germany are yellow, whereas in the United Kingdom they are red. Only if the color is correct will the viewer easily identify it as a mailbox. > FIG. 3 This is generally taken into account in weather maps, with a few exceptions. Oceans, lakes, and rivers are blue; forests and meadows are green; mountainous regions are brown in the valleys and white on the peaks. In addition, aggregate states – e.g., hot (red) or cold (blue) – can be indicated by colors. <

/ C2.2.4
MULTIDIMENSIONALITY

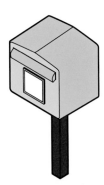

FIG. 3
German mailbox in yellow
British mailbox in red

C 2.2 / ANIMATING COLORS

C 2.2.1 / COLOR CODING

Color coding is one of the most basic applications for color in information design and hence for possibilities of its use that are presented below. For example, an object can be given meaning by assigning it a color. A common example of this is indicating that it belongs to a certain group. Regions, areas, elements, or objects can be colored with an animation and categorized in this way.

This is a common practice in graphics for elections. Over the course of the evening of the election, precincts that have been won by a given party are colored in with the corresponding color on a map. Precincts previously ruled by a different party change color when taken by a competing party. Hence the color coding changes along with the temporal context. This kind of dynamic process can be very illustrated with an animation. > **FIG. 4**

To ensure that the viewer can distinguish all categories right away very distinct colors should be used to represent them.

TUFTE and WARE agree on this: a large number of colors should be avoided in comparisons. Moreover, the colors of the visible light spectrum (red, orange, yellow, green, blue, indigo, and violet) should be avoided. Even though they ensure changes in color of equal distance, they are poor in terms of ergonomics. No hierarchy or meaning can be conveyed by them.

In an analysis of colors on German television and elsewhere, we studied how many colors are employed on average in an information graphic. The subjects of the study were statistics, maps, and functional graphics on news broadcasts and in science magazines. We observed the colors of the significant elements and found that the elements studied were encoded with two to four colors. In practice, then, a considerably smaller number of colors are used in practice than TUFTE and WARE recommend for static images. The reduction of color as a variable is a response to the availability of additional variables, such as time, animation, and voice over, which in combination can quickly overwhelm an animation.

FIG. 4

It makes sense to employ no more than four colors for significant elements.

The principle is that differentiating and categorizing elements requires a certain attention span – a valuable commodity in a time-based, moving medium.

If more ways of differentiating are necessary, however, then it is best to make use of formal elements, which can also facilitate good selection. When this is no solution, one should ask whether the data set or state of affairs to be animated is really suitable for a moving image, given its complexity. Perhaps it needs to be broken down into subsequences, each of which has its own clear core message. ‹

/ B2.1
CORE MESSAGE

C 2.2.2 / GROUPING BY COLOR

Grouping by color is the logical extension of color coding. As mentioned above in the context of color dominance, colors are more easily perceived as a selection and faster to grasp than forms. ‹ Correspondingly, viewers perceive elements with the same color as belonging together and can therefore assign them to a given category more easily. > FIG. 5

/ C2.1.1
COLOR DOMINANCE

In an animation, elements can expand or change according to a temporally or otherwise changing context and in a way that is visually traceable and therefore easy to follow by the viewer.

In the detail of a map in FIG. 6, the separate areas are perceived as belonging together despite being separated spatially and having different forms, so they can be assigned to the relevant category.

FIG. 5
The falling dice are assigned to categories based on color.

With one glance, the viewer can associate the various categories with the same color.

Although the forms differ in this example, the color makes it very clear they belong together, which corroborates the earlier remark that color is stronger than form.

C 2.2.3 / COLOR GRADATIONS

In addition to color coding significant elements, the gradation of a color can also convey information. It can help illustration hierarchical and quantitative orders. Animation can also clarify the temporal development of such orders. > FIG. 7

Color gradation can fulfill the function of establishing a hierarchy when illustrating rankings, for example. For even if the different color gradations do not enable one to determine exact ratios of numbers (e.g., this is one-quarter of that), they can at least provide a good overview of a distribution of values or a change in value that could scarcely be conveyed any other way.

Like the use of colors in animated information graphics in general, however, the number of gradations in a moving image should be limited.

Experiences with various render/codecs on different distribution media have shown that a 25 percent gradation of a color value makes sense.

FIG. 7
The circles that split off are rendered in the same color spectrum as the original so they can be clearly recognized as a variation of it.

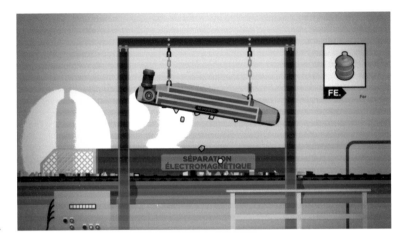

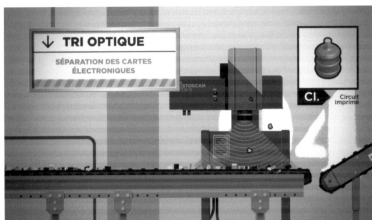

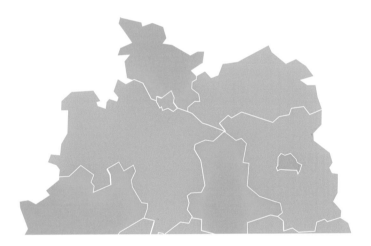

FIG. 6

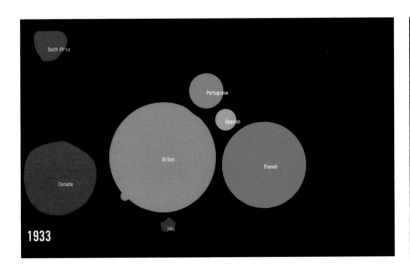

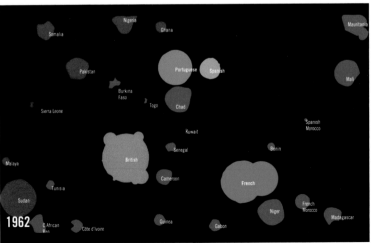

C 2.2.4 / MULTIDIMENSIONALITY

In addition to the ordering functions mentioned, colors can be granted a symbolic power as a result of elements with other levels of meaning. This quality is generally summed up with the term multidimensionality and can be educationally effective in animations.

In Western cultures, for example, red can signify danger but also love; green often stands for safety and positivity; blue for cold; and white for clarity. Many of these color codes are deeply rooted in conventions and common sense. For example, changing the color of a stop sign to green would have fatal consequences. Several colors are, of course, laden with such meaning.

Changing the color in an animation can thus give an element a different meaning. This can be particularly useful for visualizations of abstract processes, such as changes in temperature. Blue can stand for cold and red for warm. Animated changes between these colors can thus communicate this change transparently and understandably.

Multidimensionality can also lead to misunderstandings. In China red stands for luck. In much of Asia, white stands for mourning, which is represented by black in Western regions. > **FIG. 8**

FIG. 8
In this case, the pulsating yellow color of the element indicates it is getting extremely hot.

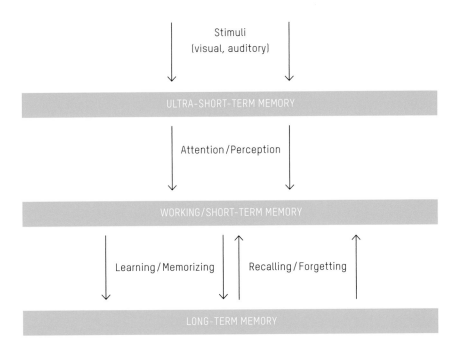

FIG. 14
Tripartite model for memory based on
the theory by Colin Ware

C 2.4 / ANIMATING FORMS

If we keep the principles of designing with reduced forms in the back of our minds, we can now devote ourselves to the animation of forms. The following chapter explains the available options for animated information graphics and what meanings they can convey.

Animating forms and the resulting change in values can be used to describe quantitative, temporal, and even physical properties. Moreover, forms in an animation can permit inferences concerning causal connections and also depict real patterns of movement.

In this context, the term form should be understood rather abstractly. For example, a form can represent any graphic construct, from the line to the three-dimensional volume.

C 2.4.1 / QUANTITY

/ C 2.2.3
COLOR GRADATIONS

In contrast to color gradations, forms offer the possibility of depicting quantities as accurate numbers. ◁ The viewer can determine from the ratio of two forms how often the one is found in the other and thus understand the ratio depicted without the actual underlying values being identified. ▷ FIG. 15

Bar charts are based on this idea, hence they are particularly suitable in short animations as a way to convey a quick impression of quantitative relationships.

When animating forms, a dynamic change in scale can illustrate variation in the underlying values.

For example, charts can show growth or stagnation within a certain time frame. In line and area charts, too, the temporal components can be illustrated by animating the curves and areas.

C 2.4.2 / CAUSALITY

Animating forms in a schematic rendering can depict causal connections between the individual forms – for example, one gear moves the other. This shows which parts are dependent on other parts of the presentation in terms of their movement, their existence, or their appearance. At first glance, that might seem obvious, but it is a unique selling point of the animated information graphic. In contrast to the printed information graphic – which can often reproduce such connections only in comic strip form or with the aid of additional graphic elements, such as arrows, to indicate the direction of movement – animation reproduces the forms directly.

Moreover, even abstract, invisible processes like depictions of ultrasonic waves can be made comprehensible with the aid of animated forms.

One little trap: an abstracted representation sometimes has little to do with its real equivalent. For example, gas does not look like smoke, as it is often depicted, and sound waves are not arranged in concentric circles. Such representations run the risk of being accepted by the viewer as fact.

Animated forms can also be employed to direct attention. In that case, the animation itself conveys no meaning but merely directs the viewer's eyes to a different section of the graphic. Here forms work to keep the focus on the point of interest. The form can be scaled, made to blink, or its opacity can be altered. > FIG. 16 & 17

C 2.4.3 / CONSTITUTION

If a ball bounces on the floor, the way it is animated makes its physical properties evident. The extent of its deformation and the speed with which it bounces back provides information about how hard the ball is. An animation is the only way to depict such a situation realistically. The depiction can be supplemented by an appropriate sound. Especially in schematic renderings illustrating how machines function, this kind of animation can be informative and make a graphic more easy to understand.

FIG. 15
Scaling the red area along the y-axis indicates a quantity.

FIG. 16
As the BMI (Body Mass Index) rises or falls, the body gets fatter or thinner. Here again the transformation of two objects reveals a direct dependence.

FIG. 17
The simultaneous animation of the wheels and the belt eveals the relationship between the individual elements.

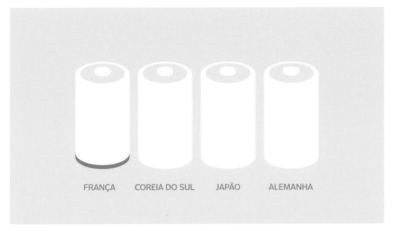

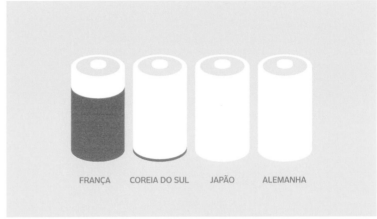

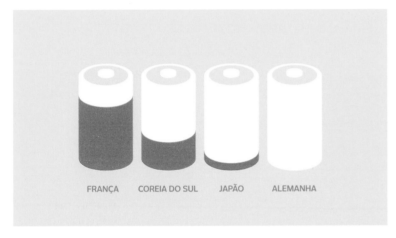

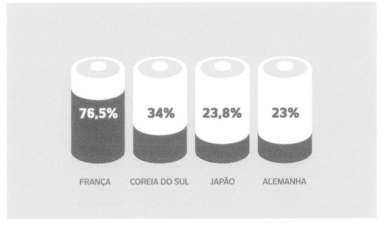

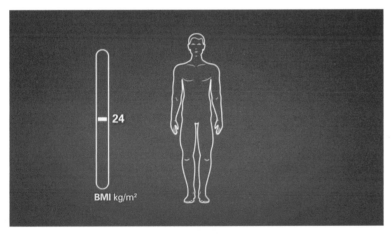

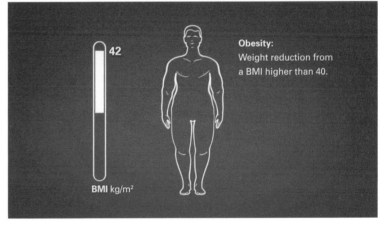

C3 /
VOICE OVER

THE VOICE OVER
REDUCES VISUAL
COMPLEXITY.

An information graphic can contain text, which either labels individual elements or directs the viewer's attention. With more complex visualizations in the medium of moving images, such as schematic renderings, it can be advantageous to explain the information graphic purely on the visual level. Frequently in such complex presentations a text level does not require a more complex understanding because the viewer is confronted with too much visual information at once. Hence, there is a risk that some information is not processed. For that reason, among others, it is advisable to employ a voice over in a design, thereby replacing texts with audio and conveying them on a second channel of perception.

Basically, a voice over is a speaker's commentary spoken over a sequence.

There are many different kinds of voice overs, and they are each used in diverse ways. For example, they are found in live sports broadcasts, news reports, off-screen voices in films, advertisements, and translations – indeed, this is only a small selection. <

Messages that combine words and images are better-anchored than those encountered exclusively in visual forms. Voice overs should not simply be regarded as a way to make complex presentations more clearly but also as a way of anchoring information more enduringly. <

To help understand the use of voice over, WINFRIED NÖTH has summarized it as follows: <

Voice overs can

/ improve the presentation of points, spaces, and sequences in time;

/ describe impressions of all sensory perceptions, not just visual ones but also acoustic, olfactory, thermal, and tactile impressions; and

/ represent the concrete as well as the abstract.

NÖTH's first point – that voice overs can better present sequences in time – supports the view that voice overs are particularly suited to conveying procedural information, as in schematic renderings. < The second and third points show that a direct added value can be obtained by adding a verbal level. For example, it can convey sense impressions that could be difficult to illustrate visually: *This surface has an antislip coating.*

However, this added value is obtained only if the voice over is clearly linked with the visualization. We will explain the possibilities for combining these two channels below. This is the only way to ensure a graphic is understood.

/ COLIN WARE
Information Visualization:
Perception for Design
p. 312

/ COLIN WARE
Information Visualization:
Perception for Design,
p. 312
/ WINFRIED NÖTH
Handbuch der Semiotik,
p. 482

/ COLIN WARE
Information Visualization:
Perception for Design,
p. 320

C 3.1 / CONTENT

The voice over can take up the content-related functions of elements in a graphic and thus allow for more space.

C 3.1.1 / LABELING BY MEANS OF VOICE OVER

One significant advantage of the voice over in information graphics is the possibility of replacing labels in the graphic or at least reducing them. This frees the graphic of visual information that can instead by conveyed via the auditory channel. Because a moving image has a more limited display area, this can save valuable space. HELMUT M. NIEGEMANN corroborates this assumption:

/ "Written texts are first processed in the visual/image channel and then switch to the auditory/verbal channel. Consequently cognitive resources from both channels have to be available to adequately process written texts." ‹

/ HELMUT M.
NIEGEMANN ET AL.
*Kompendium
multimediales
Lernen,*
p. 52

When employing this technique it is necessary to make a selection of words: first because the capacity of the channels is limited; and second, because the viewer actively selects the most important words.

The voice over can, however, also be used to supplement text labeling in order to better anchor the corresponding information.

The aforementioned requirement that voice over and visualization must have a direct relationship applies to labeling as well.

FIG. 1
The Dual Coding Theory by PAVIO

If a voice over and text labeling are employed in parallel, the text of a label should also be mentioned in the voice over when the label appears.

Deviating from this rule can result in confusion. When the content of the label differs from that of the voice over, it can result in irritating the viewer. These brief thinking pauses inevitably lead to the information that immediately follows getting lost.

C 3.1.2 / MENTAL IMAGES

In his article "Concrete Image and Verbal Memory Codes," ALLAN PAIVIO proposes the thesis that information is stored in our working memory in two different ways. < He calls these two ways imagens and logogens. Imagens are mental representations of verbal information; logogens is his term for mental representations of visual information. This illustration explains this *dual coding theory*: > **FIG. 1**

Mental images are produced, for example, when a dialogue tries to compare the green of a kiwi with the green of a Christmas tree, or to compare the size of a lightbulb with that of a tennis ball. <

The theory of mental images opens up a broad spectrum for the voice over, and it demonstrates that we are able to bring words into a visual context.

/ MEDIALINE
tinyurl.com/d6xahyh

/ COLIN WARE
Information Visualization:
Perception for Design,
p. 312

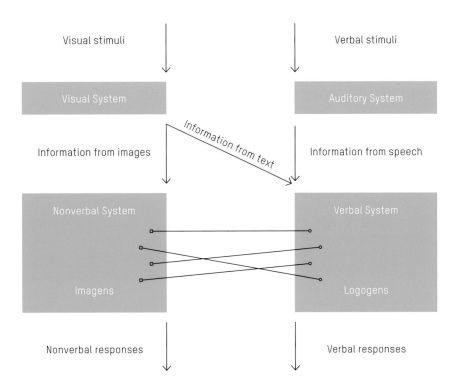

C 3.2 / POINT IN TIME

In addition to the proper balance of language and image, the temporal connection of both channels is also very important.

Studies by PETER FARADAY and ALISTAIR SUTCLIFFE have shown that a direct linkage of text and image results in better understanding. < There are two different ways to connect text/language and image: statically, between text and image (e.g., labeling in diagrams) and dynamically, between language and image (voice overs in animations). <

/ PETER FARADAY,
ALISTAIR SUTCLIFFE
Authoring Animated
Web Pages Using
"Contact Points"
/ B 3.2
LABELING

The example in FIG. 1 shows how linking image with spoken text should be achieved. At precisely the moment when the voice over names the object located in the point of interest, it is also emphasized in the graphic. This direct linking of auditory and verbal channels maximizes the anchoring in the viewer's head.

C 3.2.1 / CONNECTION

PETER FARADAY and ALISTAIR SUTCLIFFE also studied when the voice over was spoken in relation to the visual event. They concluded that the visual event should appear simultaneously with the voice over. <

/ SIGCHI.ORG
tinyurl.com/d9pwl2q

The effectiveness and application of this point were tested in an analysis. The subject of the study was information graphics in news programs and science programs on German television.

The study examined 46 reports with a total of 242 situations in which a visual event occurred with a verbal one.

The result in FIG. 2 shows a positive tendency but also a lot of missed potential. In (A) 131 events occurred simultaneously with a voice over; in (B) 43 events were too early; and in (C) 59 events were too late. In (D) 9 visual events were not even mentioned in the voice over.

Taking into account the fact that the voice overs of news broadcasts are not produced exclusively for the visualization but rather spoken live by the newscaster, our analysis shows that there is an effort to ensure the two are simultaneous.

C 3.2.2 / DEICTIC GESTURE

If one points to an object when speaking, this link is called deictic gesture. For example, if someone points to her new boat while talking about it, the link is created by her hand. This method can be observed daily in weather reports and is therefore probably the most common one. Even small children make use of this gesture when they speak. > FIG. 3

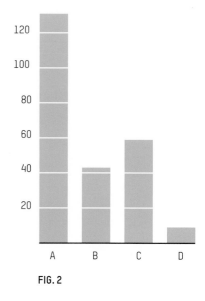

FIG. 2

FIG. 3
The deictic gesture was used even in the early days of animated information graphics: in the form of a pointer.

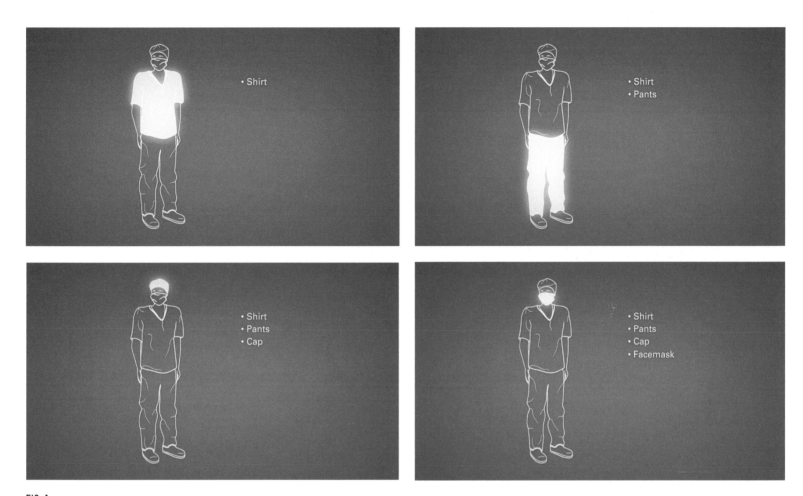

FIG. 1

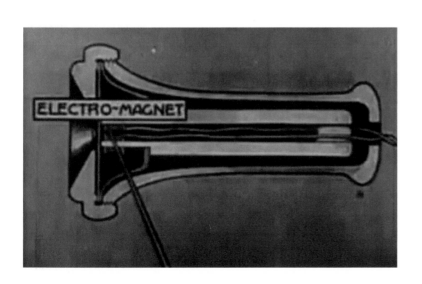

C 3.3 / RELATIONSHIPS

Here is a list of three different possibilities for combining words and images.

C 3.3.1 / COMPLEMENTARITY

Complementarity is the ideal way to combine words with images. Both sources of information are necessary to grasp the overall meaning. The text and the image are both incomplete by themselves and they supplement each other with their media-specific potential as each fills the other's gaps. This criterion can overlap with those of dominance and redundancy since the extent of such supplements can vary from case to case. > FIG. 4

C 3.3.2 / DOMINANCE

Dominance can refer either to text or images. The dominant part can stand alone, as it does not need the other part to be understood. One can speak of visual dominance "if an idea of the thing sketched would be difficult to obtain without the image." < In the case of text dominance, the image illustrates; it decorates the text or seems didactic. > FIG. 5

KLAUS BRINKER
*Text- und
Gesprächslinguistik,*
p. 493

C 3.3.3 / REDUNDANCY

Redundancy is the opposite of dominance. The image corresponds to the spoken text and it illustrates the textual information. Equality on both channels leads to a simultaneous processing of information. According to WARE, this makes it more effective, but it also runs the risk of becoming monotonous. < > FIG. 6

/ C 3.2
POINT IN TIME

FIG. 4

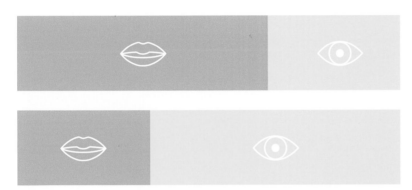

FIG. 5

FIG. 6

C4/
SOUND

SOUND CAN HELP
PUT DEPICTIONS OR
VISUAL EVENTS
INTO CONTEXT.

There are three requirements for the existence of a sound. First, there must be a source that emits the sound. Then, the acoustic energy has to be conveyed via a medium such as air or water. Finally, it has to reach a microphone or an ear. As soon as the impulse has entered the ear, the brain transforms it into sound, which is a subjective interpretation.

As with the voice over, there are various ways of combining sound with a visualization.

If the sound is heard by the actor − e.g., in a film − and the viewer, it is called *diegetic*. The sound can thus be located in the space and time of the action. ‹ If that is not possible, and the sound is heard only by the viewer, then it is called *nondiegetic*. Diegetic sounds either have a source that is visually present, in which case it is called an *on-screen* sound, or one that is not, in which case it is an *off-screen* sound. An *active* off-screen sound is one the characters in the film react to. A *passive* off-screen merely contributes to the atmosphere of the image. ‹

/ MEDIENSERVER
UNIVERSITY OF HALLE
tinyurl.com/c6guk48

/ MEDIENSERVER
UNIVERSITY OF HALLE
tinyurl.com/c6guk48

Off-screen sounds are often used to stimulate the viewer's imagination to create an autonomous visualization.

The sound then becomes a narrative element. This can be illustrated well with the example of a radio drama. For example, if we hear the sound of typing on keyboards, our mind's eye pictures an office or workplace. The sound component alone is enough to establish the setting of a whole scene.

Thanks to this quality of sound, we can even create images that would be difficult to imagine on a purely visual level.

Using such off-screen sounds can be a considerable advantage in animated information graphics.

Off-screen sounds can reduce visual complexity, conveying information via the auditory channel and thus saving valuable space in the display area.

For viewers to generate an image to go with the sound, the various patterns must be stored in their memory. They are then assigned to the sound patterns. ‹

/ ROBIN BEAUCHAMP
Designing Sound for Animation,
p. 22

C 4.1 / CAUSAL SOUNDS

Sounds are *causal* if they have a cause and an effect: a cow is seen and a cow is heard. This is a category of elemental significance for some animations, especially if they depict reality.

Causal sounds are particularly well suited to schematic presentations. For example, if the mechanism of a connector is shown, it is difficult to visualize whether it is a magnet or a simple plug-in connector. A sound makes it easier to understand. > FIG. 1

C 4.2 / ACOUSMATIC SOUNDS

If a sound cannot be assigned to a source because the source is not visible, it is called an acousmatic sound. Often such sounds are transformed, forming the basis of the sound scheme for another object.

This is well suited to cartographic or statistical renderings as a way to direct stimuli by means of recurring sound elements.

A causal sound can also become acousmatic if the object that produced the sound leaves the so-called stage. The advantage of this is that from that point onward the viewer will associate the sound with the object even though it is no longer seen. That enables the designer to reduce the density of visual information and convey information on the auditory level.

Employing sound in information graphics is helpful only to a limited extent. Seen from the perspective of BERTIN, sound can be an additional variable that contributes to longer-term retention of the corresponding information. Sound as a means of design can provide a significant functional component that, just like a voice over, can relieve the burden on the visual level and thus reduce the density of data, which in the long run can improve understanding. < > FIG. 2

/ C 3
VOICE OVER

There is, however, a risk of overloading the animation, which can make it more difficult for viewers to assign the sounds to corresponding visual events.

Sounds should be employed consciously to support a process or to guide stimuli actively. <

/ C 5.5
FOCUSING THE VIEWER'S
ATTENTION VIA SOUND

/ "In a film, an acousmatic situation can develop in two different scenarios: either a sound is visualized first, and subsequently acousmatized, or it is acousmatic to start with, and it is visualized only afterwards." <

/ MICHEL CHION
*Audio-Vision:
Sound on Screen,*
p. 74

FIG. 1
When sound is combined with a visual event it directs more attention to that event.
The broadcast source is shifted to the point of interest by scaling an outline in combination with an acousmatic sound.

FIG. 2
Increasing engine noises support the visual representation of car and airplane traffic, shifting a part of information to the auditory level.

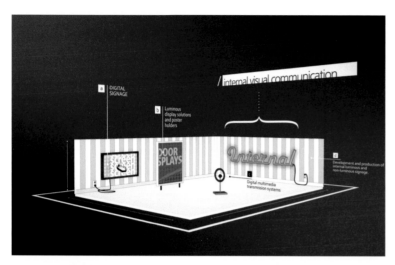

C5 /
FOCUSING THE VIEWER'S ATTENTION

ONLY ONE OBJECT SHOULD BE THE POINT OF INTEREST AT ANY GIVEN TIME.

In contrast to classic applications in print media, with an animated information graphic the viewer has a limited time to perceive the relevant information. In order to use this time as efficiently as possible and to convey the information smoothly, attention must always be focused on the significant part of the graphic.

The following chapter explains how the designer can achieve this goal by focusing the viewer's attention.

The human being has five senses:
/ **Sight** (visual perception)
/ **Hearing** (auditory perception)
/ **Smell** (olfactory perception)
/ **Taste** (gustatory perception)
/ **Touch** (tactile perception)

We can take in information via these five different channels. The distance senses of sight and hearing are important for the animated information graphic, since the information is perceived through them.

The following chapter explains how information can be most efficiently divided up among the channels. <

/ ROLAND MANGOLD
Informationspsychologie,
p. 39

C 5.1 / SACCADES

The human eye can only see a fragment of its visual field clearly, which is why we scan our surroundings with three to five saccades every second. The brain controls these leaps of the eye and brings these individual images together into an overall impression.

A perceived image disintegrates after a certain time and resolves into a uniformly gray surface. By limiting the visual field of the experimental subjects to just one detail of their visual surrounding, studies with mirrors and lenses illustrate that saccades are necessary to maintain visual perception.

Saccades are categorized by distinguishing between three different types of eye movement: jerky ones that result when scanning one side; regular, calm ones, for example, when an object moves into the field of vision slowly and the eyes have time to fixate on it; and finally, converging eye movements when an object comes directly toward us. Devices to record eye movements show that we have preferred directions when scanning: first from left to right and then diagonally from top left to bottom right. <

/ BIRGIT GURTNER, KARIN
KAINEDER, HEIKE SPERLING
Reduktion, Interaktion,
Bewegtbild,
p. 39

Saccades are centrally important to animated information graphics. Within a fixed time span, the viewer's gaze has to be focused on the significant elements, moving them to the viewer's point of interest[1]. To that end, the human eye should be encouraged to leap by something that focuses attention.

The designer has various means available to focus attention. The viewer's attention can be focused by means of colors, forms, and camera angles in combination with animations, or by means of sound and voice over.

Just as significant elements of an information graphic have to be distinguished from the background, the corresponding focus of information has to stand out from its surroundings in order to be perceived as clearly as possible. The property of the focus offered is the decisive factor here. If it stands out clearly from the rest of the graphic as a result of its color, or if it is the first thing to appear within the display area, it will very certainly be perceived first and foremost as well.

The following sections provide an overview of the possibilities available to the designer to ensure the viewer's gaze is always on the correct part of the graphic. The categories should be understood as a means of orientation. In practice, the various ways of focusing attention are combined, and in some cases they are not necessarily even required.

FIG. 1
The arrows moving up and down direct the viewer's eye to these places.

C 5.2 / FOCUSING THE VIEWER'S ATTENTION VIA MOVEMENT

Moving elements attract our eyes as if by magic, instinctively focusing our attention. Animated advertising banners on websites take advantage of this effect to attract the viewer's eye. If movement is overused, however, the gaze will turn away after a time. This also happens if the movement is perceived as regular and repetitive. Human attention is not tied to a single focus; rather, people are always prepared to turn to other focuses. A lasting, regular repetition of the animation, as found with advertising banners, for example, is often irritating to the viewer and hence distracts from the real information. Hence it is not animation alone but its targeted use that focuses successfully the viewer's attention. <

/ ROLAND MANGOLD
Informationspsychologie,
p. 85

The other ways of focusing the viewer's attention discussed here are all based on this consideration. Only focuses employed in a targeted way will successfully redirect the viewer's gaze. > FIG. 1

---

1   Point of interest: The point of interest, abbreviated POI, describes the significant part of an animated information graphic that must be in the viewer's focus at a given time in order to convey the information correctly.

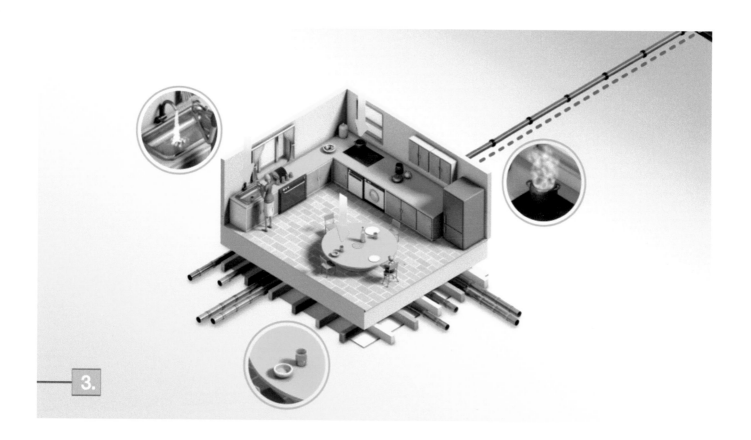

3.

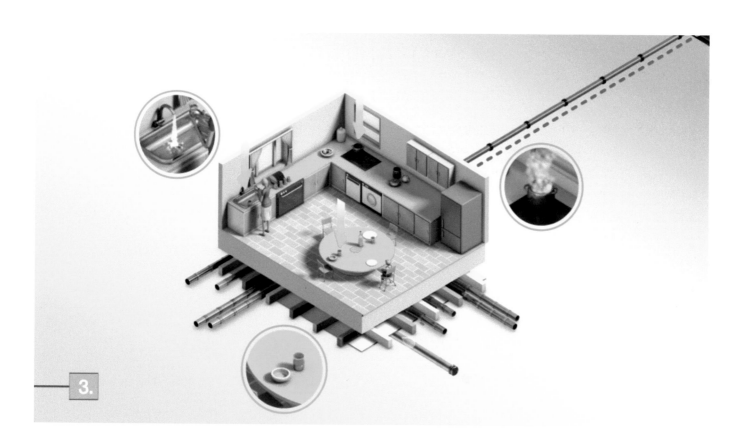

3.

C 5.3 / FOCUSING THE VIEWER'S ATTENTION VIA COLOR

Colorful focuses are more effective than black-and-white ones.

When choosing the color of a focus, it is important to pay attention to the colors of the other elements and of the background. <

/ C 2.2.1
COLOR CODING

The following possibilities are available to the designer to focus attention by means of color:

/ **Blinking** / Changing the color or the gradations of color
/ **Softening** / Desaturation of the colors of surrounding elements
/ **Coloring** / The point of interest is replaced by a stimulating color

When choosing among these options, legibility and applicability must be considered in each case.

C 5.3.1 / BLINKING

Blinking refers to changing the shade or gradation within a shade. It is primarily useful for small focuses, for example, marking sites on maps. Thus an object can blink in order to attract attention and thus become the point of interest. Two or three changes are enough to direct the viewer's eye to the desired object or corresponding section of a graphic. The time between changing colors should be no more than half a second. < > **FIG. 2**

/ FRANK THISSEN
Screen-Design Handbuch,
p. 133

C 5.3.2 / SOFTENING

Softening here means desaturating the color of the areas around the point of interest. The point of interest retains its color fully. This method for focusing attention is particularly well suited to schematic renderings. Softening the other elements of a graphic can also be used to shift the point of interest in a line chart, for example. > **FIG. 3**

C 5.3.3 / COLORING

Coloring the point of interest is well suited for use on maps, for example. Large areas (countries) can be emphasized in this way.

This means of focusing attention is not as well suited for schematic depictions where the actual color is important to understand the graphic because it would distort the picture. > **FIG. 4**

FIG. 2
Blinking indicates the area that the zoom will enlarge in a moment, directing the viewer's eye there.

FIG. 3
The slow darkening of the other areas focuses the viewer's eye on the point of interest.

FIG. 4
The stark contrast of the colored areas draws the viewer's eye.

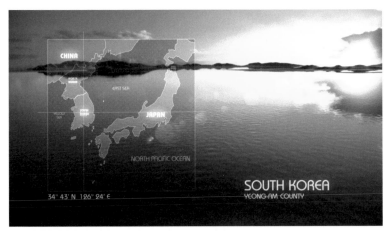

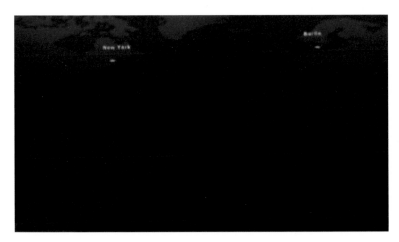

187

C 5.4 / FOCUSING THE VIEWER'S ATTENTION VIA FORM

Forms can emphasize areas or announce a zoom.

The following possibilities are available to the designer for focusing attention via form:

/ **Scaling** / Rhythmically changing an object's size
/ **Outlining** / Demarcating an area
/ **Marking** / Emphasizing a point with a form

C 5.4.1 / SCALING

Scaling a form, e.g., increasing a marking within a graphic, can be used to direct the viewer's eye to a form and thus shift an object to the point of interest. It is also possible to rhythmically repeat the scaling to keep the viewer focused on the object.
> FIG. 5

C 5.4.2 / OUTLINING

Outlining is a useful method because it covers up visualizations as little as possible. Its effect can also be heightened by animating it slightly using scaling. Outlining is suitable for indicating circles or radii on maps, for example.
> FIG. 6

C 5.4.3 / MARKING

Marking is used to indicate a point on a map. A clear geometric figure (square, triangle, circle) should be used. It can also be used in combination with blinking.
> FIG. 7

FIG. 5
Scaling the circular area beneath the figure places it in the point of interest.

FIG. 6
The outline marks the point of interest. The strong contrast between the foreground (outline) and background attracts attention even more effectively.

FIG. 7
Geo-located tweets are shown as yellow circles that fade away with time.

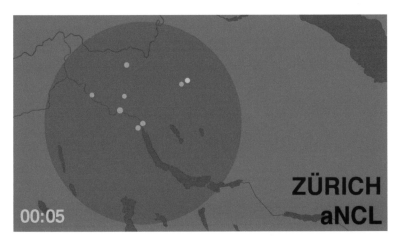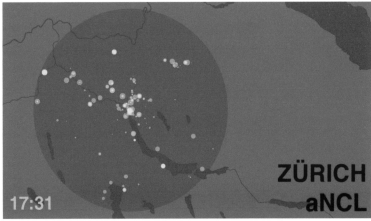

C 5.5 / FOCUSING THE VIEWER'S ATTENTION 🖵 VIA SOUND

Visual events can be reinforced in the viewer's perception by combining them with sounds.

Sound occupies a special place among the ways of focusing attention. In contrast to visual means of focusing attention or the voice over, it is not possible to direct attention to a particular part of a graphic by means of sound alone. That is because it is not initially possible to localize sound in a space. Even with stereophony,[2] only rough directional indications of left versus right are possible, but they are too imprecise to make sound an effective means of focusing attention on their own. Only in combination with other means does sound produce its reinforcing effect. Basically, it is important to ensure that the sound is always directly linked to, or is shown simultaneously with, the corresponding visual focus so that the viewer can connect them clearly. If this is not done effectively, one runs the risk of confusion, misinterpretation and loss of information. ‹

/ COLIN WARE:
Information Visualization:
Perception for Design,
p. 363

Sounds, much like animations, should only be employed in a way that contributes to understanding or temporarily reduces other atmospheric sound elements in order for them to focus attention effectively.

When choosing a sound, one has to decide between an artificially produced sound and a real sound that could be associated with the object in question. This depends on the nature of visualization, of course. An animation of an abstract form, such as a circle, should have an abstract/artificial sound. If it is a real object, it can be combined with a corresponding real sound, which also helps to describe the object.

C 5.6 / FOCUSING THE VIEWER'S ATTENTION 🖵 VIA VOICE OVER

Voice over can name or enumerate visual events and thus make them the point of interest.

FIG. 8
The words "into the wound area" in the voice over draw attention to the wound area. In this example, the voice over supports the movement of the arrow.

---

2 *Stereophony* is used to describe technologies that create a spatial impression of sound by means of at least two sound sources (e.g., loudspeakers).

Directional instructions and other forms of voice over offer a variety of ways to guide the viewer's eye: "The power switch is underneath the device." It can also identify visual properties of significant elements: "Pressing and holding the red button will restart the computer." Finally, it can shift objects to the visual focus: "The smallest model is also the most affordable of those illustrated here." > FIG. 8

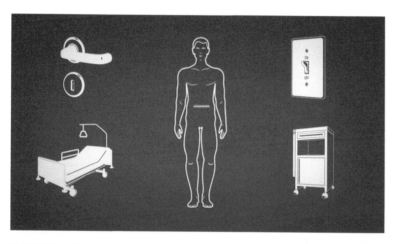
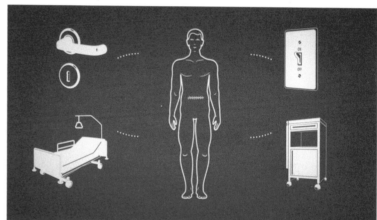
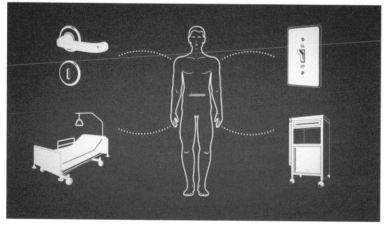
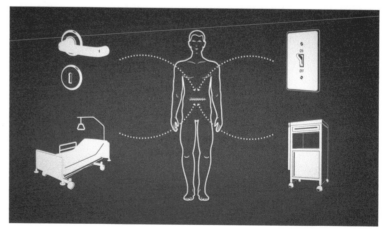

C 5.7 / FOCUSING THE VIEWER'S ATTENTION VIA CAMERA

The camera also offers ways to direct the viewer's eye. A zoom, a tracking shot, or a change in the depth of field can be employed.

C 5.7.1 / ZOOM

A *zoom* is expedient when one wants to offer a detailed view. The zoom has the added advantage that parts of the visualization that are not important at that moment are moved out of focus. Hence the viewer can concentrate entirely on the significant elements of the graphic and unnecessary saccades are avoided. > **FIG. 9**

C 5.7.2 / TRACKING

Much like a zoom, a *tracking shot* makes the relevant parts of a graphic the viewer's focus. It can *track* various areas of an object or map, thereby making processes evident. The use of appropriate camera angles should also be considered. < > **FIG. 10**

/ C 1.3
CAMERA ANGLES

C 5.7.3 / DEPTH OF FIELD

Changing the *depth of field* works similarly to softening elements outside the point of interest. The sharply focused elements of the graphic are shifted to the point of interest, while blurry ones are moved out of it.

FIG. 9
By zooming out, the view moves from the detail to the whole situation without losing the overview.

FIG. 10
The camera tracks the various areas, each of which is in turn the point of interest. In order to avoid distortion, the camera should always be at a 90 degree angle to the display area.

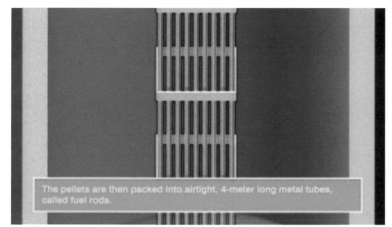

The pellets are then packed into airtight, 4-meter long metal tubes, called fuel rods.

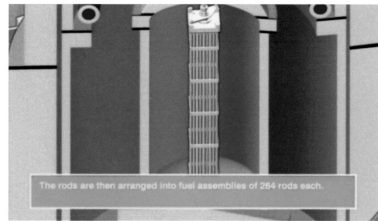

The rods are then arranged into fuel assemblies of 264 rods each.

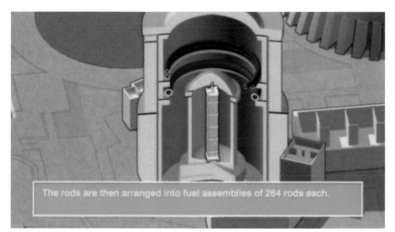

The rods are then arranged into fuel assemblies of 264 rods each.

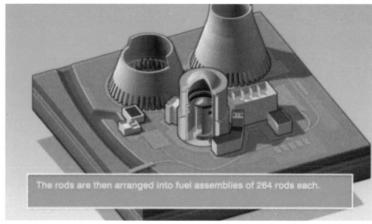

The rods are then arranged into fuel assemblies of 264 rods each.

DEATH ROW

Sect 04.5

Sect 04.6

Number of p

Number of prisoners executed by
the U.S. Government since 1976.

xecuted by
ince 1976.

1,1,3,6,

Official

Numb
deat

D/

/CONTENT

ADDENDUM

D1 / BIBLIOGRAPHY

AUER GRAFIKDIENST

"Infografik: Die optische Sprache." www.auer.at. Accessed December 12, 2011.

BEAUCHAMP, ROBIN

Designing Sound for Animation. Oxford, UK: Butterworth Heinemann, 2005.

BEHRENS, CHRISTIAN

"The Form of Facts and Figures." Master's thesis. *www.niceone.org.*

BERTIN, JACQUES

Semiology of Graphics: Diagrams, Networks, Maps. Translated by William J. Berg.
Madison: Univ. of Wisconsin Press, 1983.

CHION, MICHEL

Audio-Vision: Sound on Screen. Edited and translated by Claudia Gorbman.
New York: Columbia Univ. Press, 1994.

DIEZMANN, TANJA, AND TOBIAS GREMMLER

Raster für das Bewegtbild / Grids for the Dynamic Image. Lausanne, Switzerland:
AVA, 2003.

FARADAY, PETER, AND ALISTAIR SUTCLIFF

"Authoring Animated Web Pages Using 'Contact Points'." *dl.acm.org/citation.
cfm?id=302979.303131.* Accessed December 12, 2011.

GURTNER, BIRGIT, KARIN KAINEDER, AND HEIKE SPERLING

*Reduktion, Interaktion, Bewegtbild: Gestalterische Grundlagen im Kontext von
Multimedialität.* Berlin: Pro Business, 2006.

HARTMANN, FRANK, AND ERWIN K BAUER

Bildersprache: Otto Neurath; Visualisierungen. 2nd exp. ed. Vienna. Facultas, 2006.

JANSEN, ANGELA, AND WOLFGANG SCHARFE

*Handbuch der Infografik: Visuelle Information in Publizistik, Werbung und
Öffentlichkeitsarbeit.* Berlin: Springer, 1999.

LIEBIG, MARTIN

Die Infografik. Constance, Germany: UVK Medien, 1999.

MANGOLD, ROLAND

Informationspsychologie, Wahrnehmen und Gestalten in der Medienwelt. Munich:
Elsevier, Spektrum Akademischer Verlag, 2007.

MAYER, RICHARD E.

Multimedia Learning. Cambridge, UK: Cambridge Univ. Press, 2001.

NIEGEMANN, HELMUT M., ET AL.

Kompendium multimediales Lernen. Berlin: Springer, 2008.

NÖTH, WINFRIED

Handbuch der Semiotik. 2nd exp. ed. Stuttgart: J. B. Metzler, 2000.

"Der Zusammenhang von Text und Bild." In Klaus Brinker, ed. *Text- und Gesprächslinguistik: Ein internationales Handbuch zeitgenössischer Forschung/ Linguistics of Text and Conversation: An International Handbook of Contemporary Research,* 489–96. Berlin: Walter de Gruyter, 2000.

PAIVIO, ALLAN, AND KAL CSAPO

"Concrete Image and Verbal Memory Codes." Journal of Experimental Psychology, 80:2, pt. 1 (May 1969): 279–85.

SPRISSLER, HANNO

Infografiken gestalten. Berlin: Springer, 1999.

THISSEN, FRANK

Screen-Design-Handbuch: Effektiv informieren und kommunizieren mit Multimedia. Berlin: Springer, 2000.

Screen Design Manual: Communicating Effectively through Multimedia. Translated by J. G. Rager. Heidelberg: Springer, forthcoming.

TUFTE, EDWARD ROLF

The Visual Display of Quantitative Information. 2nd ed. Cheshire, CT: Graphics, 2004.

Envisioning Information. 8th printing. Cheshire, CT: Graphics, 2001.

WARE, COLIN

Information Visualization: Perception for Design. San Francisco: Morgan Kaufmann, 2000.

Visual Thinking for Design. Burlington, MA: Morgan Kaufmann, 2008.

D 2 / CREDITS

3-D ANIMATIONS, PROFILES, AND GRAPHICS FOR THE TOUR DE FRANCE
CLIENT Saarländischer Rundfunk (ARD) / PRODUCTION terra media services
/ HEAD OF PRODUCTION, DIRECTOR, AND CREATIVE DIRECTOR Kathrin Pfau
/ 3-D ARTIST (ANIMATION) Uwe Hannig
/ COMPOSITING AND SOUND DESIGN Stephan Boehme
/ GRAPHICS Martin Anner / GEODATA PROCESSING Dr. Svetlana Simonis
/ TECHNICAL DIRECTION OF 3-D RENDERING Dieter Eble
/ WEB *www.terra-media-services.de*

61 SHOTS
HEAD OF PROJECT Juan Ramos / CONCEPT Ángeles López, Juan Ramos
/ INFORMATION RESEACH Miguel Nuño
/ INFORMATION ASSISTANT David Alameda
/ CHARACTER ANIMATION David Alegre
/ VIDEO PRODUCTION Ángeles López, Juan Ramos, David Alegre
/ AUDIO PRODUCTION Manuel Arias / VOICE Gonzalo Estefanía
/ WEB *www.61shots.com*

A /

ANCL – ZURICH TWITTER TRAFFIC
Anders Johansson / WEB *www.ajohansson.com*

ATLANTIS
DESIGNED & ANIMATED BY Rod Lord
/ PRODUCED BY Myriad Global Media for BP America
/ WEB *www.rodlord.com*

ARD MAPS ON EVENT-SPACE / WEATHERMAPS
ORIGINATOR ARD-aktuell / Tagesschau

B /

BACK TO THE START
CLIENT Chipotle / AGENCY CAA and Chipotle
/ Production Company / NEXUS DIRECTOR Johnny Kelly
/ NEXUS EXEC PRODUCER Cedric Gairard , Chris O'Reilly, Charlotte Bavasso

/ NEXUS PRODUCER Liz Chan

/ NEXUS PRODUCTION MANAGER Clair Thompson, Alistair Pratten

/ DIRECTOR OF PHOTOGRAPHY Matt Day / CAMERA ASSISTANT Max Halstead

/ CHARACTER ANIMATOR Gary Cureton / SET ANIMATOR Matt Cooper

/ COMPOSITORS Alasdair Brotherston, John Taylor

/ 3D PREVIS LEAD Mark Davies / PRODUCTION DESIGNER Graham Staughton

/ ART DEPARTMENT Gordon Allen, Ben Côté, Joe Kirton

/ STUDIO MANAGER Elizabeth Day / MODELS Bob @ Artem

/ MUSIC SUPERVISION David Leinhardt at Duotone Audio

/ MUSIC PRODUCERS Justin Stanley and Doyle Bramhall

/ CONTENT MANAGER Liz Graves / ARTIST Willie Nelson

/ SOUND DESIGN Barnaby Templer @ Fonic / MODEL ASSISTANT Joe James

/ ELECTRICIAN Aldo Camileri / MODEL RIGGER Gary Faulkner

/ WEB www.nexush.com

BIRDS VS. PLANES

CLIENT Discovery Channel Latinamerica / US Hispanics

/ DIRECTOR Maximiliano Vaccaro

/ CREATIVE DIRECTION & DESIGN Juan Martin Cucurulo

/ EXECUTIVE PRODUCTION Agustin Gomez Vega

/ ANIMATION Jorge Herrero

/ RESEARCH & SCRIPTING Mario Tobelem / WEB www.noblink.tv

BT — LONGTERM INVESTOR

BT — PROPERTY VS. SHARES

CLIENT BT Financial

/ CONCEPT, WRITING & ART DIRECTION BY The Glue Society

/ DIRECTION BY The Glue Society / AGENCY Host

/ PRODUCTION BY Revolver / CINEMATOGRAPHY BY Russell Boyd ACS ASC

/ WEB www.gluesociety.com

C /

CANAL ISABEL II — THE WATER CYCLE

CLIENT Canal Isabel II / AGENCY binalogue / MUSIC Claudio Bonaldi

/ WEB www.binalogue.com

CENTRO DE LA TIERRA

CLIENT Discovery Channel Latinamerica / US Hispanics

/ DIRECTOR Maximiliano Vaccaro / WEB www.noblink.tv

FIG. 3 > p. 175   COMMUNICATION: A FILM LESSON IN GENERAL SCIENCE / DEVELOPMENT OF
COMMUNICATION

AUTHOR unknown

p. 74, 75   CGA — CANADA WEST JET

CLIENT Certified General Accountants / ADVERTISING AGENCY Grip Ltd.
/ PARTNER, CREATIVE Bob Goulart / PARTNER, CREATIVE Dave Hamilton
/ GROUP ACCOUNT DIRECTOR, BUSINESS Lauren Michell
/ MANAGER, BUSINESS Sylvie Chicoine
/ AGENCY PRODUCER, BROADCAST Jennifer Cursio
/ PRODUCTION COMPANY Sons and Daughters / DIRECTOR Barney Cokeliss
/ EXEC. PRODUCER Liane Thomas / DOP Jonny Cliff / EDITORIAL COMPANY Bijou
/ EDITOR Ross Birchall / VISUAL EFFECTS / CG / DESIGN Crush Inc.
/ CREATIVE DIRECTOR Gary Thomas / EXEC. PRODUCER Patty Bradley
/ SENIOR FLAME ARTIST David Whiteson / SENIOR DESIGNER Julia Deakin
/ SENIOR CG ANIMATOR Chris Minos / CG ARTIST Josh Clifton
/ CG ARTIST Leo Silva / WEB *www.griplimited.com*

D /

FIG. 7 > p. 153   DU BIST TERRORIST

DIRECTION Alexander Lehmann / MUSIC Iambic
/ VOICE OVER E.W. Siemon / WEB *www.alexanderlehmann.net*

p. 32, 33   DUELITY

DIRECTION, DESIGN, ANIMATION Ryan Uhrich *(ryanu.tv)*, Marcos Ceravolo
(bocamotion.tv)
/ CONCEPT Ryan Uhrich, Marcos Ceravolo, Sergio Toporek, Sebastien De Castell,
Mark Busse
/ SOUND DESIGN Chris Ray *(myspace.com / abacusrecords)*, James Boatman
/ MUSICAL SCORE Chris Ray / WRITTEN BY Lee Henderson *(leehenderson.com)*
/ ADVISORS Sergio Toporek *(shop.toporek.com)* and Mark Busse *(industrialbrand.com)*
/ VOICE OVER Rob Wood and Mariem Henaine *(linkedin.com / in / mariemhenaine)*
/ SPECIAL THANKS Sebastien De Castell
/ PRODUCED AT Vancouver Film School *(vfs.com)* (2007) / WEB *www.ryanu.tv*

E /

EMPIRES DECLINE – REVISITED

AUTHOR Pedro Cruz (CISUC)

/ SUPERVISORS Penousal Machado (CISUC) & João Bicker (FBA)

(CISUC – Centre for Informatics and Systems of the University of Coimbra)

/ WEB *www.pmcruz.com*

ESCALATOR

SERIES Factory Floor with Marshall Brain

/ ANIMATION PACKAGE PRODUCED BY Betatron Studios *(betatronstudios.com/blog)* / CREATIVE DIRECTOR R. Scott Purcell / PRODUCER EDITOR Bob Larkin

/ LEAD CG ARTIST / ANIMATION Joel Dubin *(joelotron.wordpress.com)*

ESI HEALTH CARE

AGENCY Neue Digitale / Razorfish

/ STORYBOARD & CONCEPT Stefan Fichtel, ixtract

/ ANIMATION & DESIGN Shape Minds Moving Images

/ WEB *www.neue-digitale.de*

EXPERTS EN ENERGIE. PRODUCTION

AGENCY H5 / PRODUCTION Addict / WEB *www.h5.fr*

F /

F1 2011 RED BULL RACING — TRACK SIMULATION GP KOREA

CLIENT Red Bull Media House GmbH – Andi Gall

/ DIRECTOR & PRODUCER Peter Clausen / VOICE OVER Sebastian Vettel

/ CREATION & PRODUCTION COMPANY Peter Clausen Film & TV Produktions-GmbH

/ LINE PRODUCER Cecilia Trück

/ MOTION DESIGN Christian Tyroller, Manuel Casasola Merkle

/ WEB *www.peterclausen.de*

F1 2011 RED BULL RACING CLIP — »MY INNER SECRETS — KERS & REARWING«

CLIENT Red Bull Media House GmbH – Andi Gall

/ DIRECTOR & PRODUCER Peter Clausen

/ CREATION & PRODUCTION COMPANY Peter Clausen Film & TV Produktions-GmbH

/ LINE PRODUCER Cecilia Trück

/ MOTION DESIGN Christian Tyroller, Manuel Casasola Merkle

/ WEB *www.peterclausen.de*

FAITES LE BON GESTE

AGENCY H5 / DIRECTOR H5 / POST-PRODUCTION H5 / WEB *www.h5.fr*

FREEBAND — THE AMBIENT LIFE

AGENCY PlusOne / DIRECTOR/DESIGNER Martijn Hogenkamp

/ CONCEPT Martijn Hogenkamp & Marcel Vrieswijk

/ PRODUCER Marcel Vrieswijk / COPYWRITER Marcel Vrieswijk

/ LEAD 3-D-ARTIST Tim van der Wiel / 3D-GENERALIST Erwin Tempelaars

/ 3-D-MODELING DOG Onno van Braam / MUSIC Lennert Busch

/ SOUND DESIGN Matthias Kiewiet / CLIENT Freeband Communication & IIPIC

Patrick Strating, Rene van Buuren and Sandra Lentfert

/ WEB www.plusoneamsterdam.com

H /

HACK FWD

AGENCY IDEO / WEB www.ideo.com

HELLMANN'S "EAT REAL, EAT LOCAL"

AGENCY Crush and Ogilvy & Mather Toronto

/ CHIEF CREATIVE OFFICER Nancy Vonk

/ ASSOCIATE CREATIVE DIRECTOR/AD Ivan Pols

/ COPYWRITER Siobhan Dempsey / DIRECTOR Steve Gordon & Crush, Toronto

/ PRODUCTION COMPANY Crush, Toronto & Sons and Daughters, Toronto

/ EXECUTIVE PRODUCERS Jo-Ann Cook, Crush & Dan Ford, Sons and Daughters

/ PRODUCERS Stephanie Pennington, Crush & Kate Dale, Sons and Daughters

/ CREATIVE DIRECTORS (CRUSH) Gary Thomas, Stefan Woronko

/ ART DIRECTOR (CRUSH) Yoho Hang Yue

/ ANIMATION/CG SUPERVISOR (CRUSH) Aylwin Fernando

/ EDITOR Kim Knight, Crush Cuts / MUSIC Pirate, Toronto

/ INTERACTIVE Dashboard, Toronto / WEB www.crushinc.com

HITCH-HIKER'S GUIDE TO THE GALAXY

DESIGNED & ANIMATED BY Rod Lord

/ PRODUCED BY Myriad Global Media for BP America

/ WEB www.rodlord.com

HISTORY OF THE INTERNET

DIRECTOR, ANIMATOR, DESIGN & SCRIPT Melih Bilgil

/ VOICE OVER Steve Taylor / TRANSLATION Karla Vesenmayer

/ SCIENTIFIC MANAGMENT Prof. Philipp Pape

/ UNIVERSITY University of Applied Sciences Mainz

/ THANKS TO Barbara Bittmann, Johannes Schatz

/ WEB www.lonja.de

p. 68, 69   HISTORY OF THE IPHONE

PROJECT COMMISSIONED BY CBS Interactive for CNET UK website / WRITTEN & DIRECTED BY Drew Stearne (CBS Interactive) / ILLUSTRATED & ANIMATED BY Simon Chong and Kathryn Wild (Headspin Media Ltd) / MUSIC courtesy of Audio Networks / WEB *www.headspinmedia.co.uk*

FIG. 1 > p. 91   HYPER ISLAND ON A WALL

ILLUSTRATION & ANIMATION Claudio Salas / STUDENT Robin Günther / AGENCY Jung / CREATIVE Christian Hammar / VOICE OVER Madeleine Fia Matsson / MUSIC AND SOUND Box Of Toys Audio / ACCOUNT MANAGER Linda Waxin / WEB *work.claudiosalas.com*

I /

p. 46, 47   IHG — WHAT IS GREEN ENGAGE?

CLIENT Intercontinental Hotels Group / AGENCY Dachis Group / WEB *www.dachisgroup.com*

FIG. 6A > p. 95
FIG. 8 > p. 162   INSIDE THE PLANT — POR DENTRO DA USINA

INFOGRAPHIC Maná E.D.I, Fábio Dias / MOTION GRAPHICS André Scatelli / WEB *www.andrescatelli.com*

K /

p. 84, 85   KATRINA

CLIENT Sprint / AGENCY Goodby, Silverstein & Partners / CO-CHAIRMAN/CREATIVE DIRECTOR Rich Silverstein / CREATIVE DIRECTOR(s) Christian Haas, Franklin Tipton / GROUP/ASSOC. CREATIVE DIRECTOR(s) Paul Stechschulte / ART DIRECTOR Rudi Anggono, Shane Fleming / COPYWRITER Will Elliott, Larry Corwin / EXECUTIVE PRODUCER Josh Reynolds / PRODUCER Rob Sondik / PRODUCTION/ANIMATION COMPANY Superfad / EP Kevin Batten / PRODUCER Danielle Hazan / CREATIVE DIRECTOR Justin Leibow / SENIOR ART DIRECTOR Kevin Lau / ART DIRECTOR Will Johnson / DESIGN/ANIMATION Kevin Lau, Will Johnson, Dylan Spears, Andy Kim, Glen Suhy, Ian Mankowski, Ergin Kuke / COMPOSITOR Claudia Yi Leon / MUSIC COMPANY Human / MUSIC PRODUCER Dan Pritikin / SOUND DESIGN COMPANY GSP Post / SOUND DESIGNER Amber Tisue / WEB *www.goodbysilverstein.com*

L /

LAKS PROJECT

CLIENT Reggio Emilia Municipality / AUTHOR TIWI / CONCEPT Nicola Bigi
/ STORYBOARD Gianluca Parisi, Marco Bagni
/ PRODUCTION Federico Riboldazzi
/ ILLUSTRATIONS Chiara Casamatti, Claudia Bettinardi, Lorenzo Clerici,
Marco Bagni / VOICEOVER Roberta Bedogni
/ MOTION Marco Bagni *(www.lostconversation.com)*
/ WEB *www.tiwi.it*

M /

MATTA — RELEASE THE FREQ

PRODUCTION, DIRECTION, DESIGN, CINEMATOGRAPHY, EDITING,
3D & ANIMATION Kim Holm / ARTIST Matta / TRACK Release The Freq
/ ALBUM Prototype / LABEL Ad Noiseam / WEB *www.kimholm.com*

MESSEAUFTRITT SINT GROUP

CLIENT Sint Group
/ DESIGN/ANIMATION/SOUND EFFECTS Marcus Eckert
/ CREATIVE DIRECTOR Federica Ariagno, Giorgio Natale
/ AGENCY Auge Headquarter / WEB *www.augehq.com*

N /

NUMERALHA FORÇA VERDE — GREEN POWER

INFOGRAPHIC Maná E.D.I, Fábio Dias / MOTION GRAPHICS André Scatelli
/ WEB *www.andrescatelli.com*

O /

OVERFISHING

PRODUCTION, DIRECTION, DESIGN Uli Henrik Streckenbach
/ VOICE OVER Hilmar Eichhorn / WEB *www.uhsless.de*

R /

FIG. 10 > p. 193   REPRIEVE

CLIENT Reprieve / AGENCY This is Real Art

/ CREATIVE DIRECTOR Paul Belford / ANIMATOR Chris Perry

/ DESIGN Sam Renwick / PROJECT MANAGER Kate Nielsen

/ WEB *www.thisisrealart.com*

S /

p. 64, 65   SATELLITES: A USER MANUAL / SECTION 05, WHY WE NEED SATELLITES

FIG. 5 > p. 95   SATELLITES: A USER MANUAL / SECTION 04, LAUNCH

CLIENT SES Astra / AGENCY SR/CP Sam Renwick

/ ANIMATORS Chris Perry, Dave Penn, Louise Miller

/ DESIGN & ILLUSTRATION Sam Renwick / COPYWRITER Gideon Todes

/ CREATIVE DIRECTOR Paul Belford / PROJECT MANAGER Kate Nielsen

/ AGENCY This is Real Art / WEB *srcp.co.uk*

p. 58, 59   STUXNET: ANATOMY OF A COMPUTER VIRUS

CLIENT ABC1 Australia / DIRECTOR Patrick Clair

/ WEB *patrickclair.blogspot.com*

p. 82, 83   SUBPRIME

DIRECTION Beeple / VIDEO Beeple / MUSIC Nobot

/ SOUND EFFECTS Kyle Vande Slunt / WEB *beeple-crap.com*

T /

p. 70, 71   TERRAFORM

CONCEPT, TEXT, DIRECTION, CUT Johannes Brückner

/ MENTORING Prof. Dr. Thomas Friedrich, Prof. Axel Kolaschnik (Hochschule

Mannheim)

/ CAMERA Teresa Gessert, Benjamin Hemer, Kristin Lauer, Michel Rabe

/ VOICE OVER Frauke Vetter / MUSIC Schneider TM, The Light 3000

p. 62, 63
FIG. 3A > p. 149   TEC MEETING 2009 — NEW PORTFOLIO MANAGEMENT

AGENCY Kircher Burkhard / CONCEPT, STORYBOARD, AND DESIGN Stefan Fichtel

/ VOICE OVER Kevin Cote / ANIMATIONS & MUSIC Shape Minds Moving Images

/ WEB *www.kircher-burkhardt.com*

THE CHASER'S "YES WE CANBERRA" (OPENING TITLES)

CLIENT Polar Productions and the Australian Broadcasting Corporation

/ MOTION DESIGNER Patrick Clair / 3D ARTIST Mick Watson

/ MUSIC Turning Studios

/ EXECUTIVE PRODUCER Julian Morrow

/ NETWORK EXECUTIVE PRODUCER Kath Earle

/ WEB *patrickclair.blogspot.com*

THE CRISIS EXPLAINER

BY Paddy Hirsch

THE EU FISHING FLEET AND ITS EFFECTS

CLIENT WWF Germany (World Wide Fund for Nature) / © WWF / AGENCY ixtract GmbH

/ CREATIVE DIRECTOR Stefan Fichtel / WEB *www.ixtract.de*

THE RED BULL AIR RACE

CLIENT Red Bull Media House GmbH – Andi Gall

/ VOICE OVER Kirby Chambliss / DIRECTOR & PRODUCER Peter Clausen /

/ CREATION & PRODUCTION COMPANY Peter Clausen Film & TV Produktions-GmbH

/ LINE PRODUCER Cecilia Trück

/ MOTION DESIGN Manuel Casasola Merkle, Christian Tyroller

/ WEB *www.peterclausen.de*

THE SEED

WRITTEN AND DIRECTED BY Johnny Kelly

/ PRODUCTION MANAGER Jo Bierton / 2D ANIMATION Michael Zauner

/ 3D ANIMATION Eoin Coughlan / COMPOSITING Alasdair Brotherston

/ PAPER MODELER Elin Svensson / ASSISTED BY Anna Benner

/ DIRECTOR OF PHOTOGRAPHY Mikolaj Jaroszewicz

/ STOP FRAME ANIMATOR Matthew Cooper / CAMERA ASSISTANT Rosemary Hill

/ LIGHTING ASSISTANT Amanda Maister / FILMED AT Clapham Road Studios

/ MUSIC BY Jape / SOUND SUPERVISOR Mike Wyeld / FOLEY ARTIST Sue Harding

/ RECORDING & MIXING Studio Fonic Sound Post Production

/ EXECUTIVE PRODUCERS Charlotte Bavasso & Chris O'Reilly

/ PRODUCER Christine Ponzevera

/ A Nexus Production / IN COLLABORATION WITH Goodby, Silverstein & Partners

/ WITH THE SUPPORT Of Adobe / © Nexus Productions Ltd 2008

/ WEB *www.nexusproductions.com*

THREE WAY STREET

VIDEO SHOOTING, EDITING, DESIGN, MOTION GRAPHIC Ron Gabriel

/ MUSIC Peter Gunn Theme by Art of Noise featuring Duane Eddy

/ WEB *blog.ronconcocacola.com*

U /

UNEXPECTED MUSCULARITY

CLIENT NDR/Arte "X:enius"

/ PRODUCTION COMPANY AVE Gesellschaft für Fernsehproduktion mbH

/ EDITORIAL Tina Roth, Eva Schmidt

/ EXECUTIVE PRODUCER Florian Karpf (AVE)

/ CREATIVE DIRECTION INFOGRAPHICS Stephan Ecks (Bitmapboogie Design Agency for Digital Communication)

/ ANIMATION & COMPOSITING INFOGRAPHICS Julian Braun, Stephan Ecks, Sebastian Manger (Bitmapboogie)

/ DIRECTOR OF PHOTOGRAPHY André Wawro

/ LIGHTING ASSISTANT Gerd Hogenfeld

/ MUSIC & SOUNDDESIGN Nina Mühlenkamp

/ HEAD OF THE EDITORIAL DEPARTMENT (WISSEN) Florian Karpf

W /

WIMBLEDON

ART DIRECTION & DESIGN Bryan Ku / AUDIO SOURCES BBC

/ WEB *www.bryanku.com*

WOMEN'S ECONOMIC OPPORTUNITY

DIRECTOR Jesse Thomas / CREATIVE DIRECTOR Mark Kulakoff

/ EXECUTIVE PRODUCER Becca Colbaugh / PRODUCER Leslie Bradshaw

WUNDFILM

CLIENT Johnson & Johnson Medical / AGENCY GebrüderBetz

/ PRODUCTION COMPANY Peppermill / SOUND Eckart Gadow

/ VOICE OVER Andreas Sparberg / WEB *www.peppermill-berlin.de*

INFORMOTION
ANIMATED
INFOGRAPHICS

/ EDITED BY TIM FINKE AND SEBASTIAN MANGER

/ CO-EDITED AND PREFACE BY STEFAN FICHTEL

/ TEXT AND LAYOUT BY TIM FINKE (FORMDUSCHE) AND SEBASTIAN MANGER

/ COVER BY FLOYD E. SCHULZE FOR GESTALTEN

/ COVER IMAGES FROM PAGES 37, 43, 73, 91, 185

/ TYPEFACES: T-STAR BY MIKA MISCHLER, FOUNDRY WWW.GESTALTENFONTS.COM;

/ ADOBE CASLON PRO BY CAROL TWOMBLY

/ PROJECT MANAGEMENT BY JULIAN SORGE FOR GESTALTEN

/ PRODUCTION MANAGEMENT BY JANINE MILSTREY FOR GESTALTEN

/ TRANSLATION BY STEPHEN MASON

/ PROOFREADING BY TRANSPARENT LANGUAGE SOLUTIONS

/ PRINTED BY EBERL PRINT, IMMENSTADT IM ALLGÄU

/ MADE IN GERMANY

/ PUBLISHED BY GESTALTEN, BERLIN 2012

/ ISBN 978-3-89955-415-1

/ FOR MORE INFORMATION, PLEASE VISIT *www.gestalten.com.*

Bibliographic information published by the Deutsche Nationalbibliothek.
The Deutsche Nationalbibliothek lists this publication in the Deutsche Nationalbibliografie; detailed bibliographic data are available online at dnb.d-nb.de

This book was printed according to the internationally accepted ISO 14001 standards for environmental protection, which specify requirements for an environmental management system.

This book was printed on paper certified by the FSC®.

Gestalten is a climate-neutral company. We collaborate with the non-profit carbon offset provider myclimate (*www.myclimate.org*) to neutralize the company's carbon footprint produced through our worldwide business activities by investing in projects that reduce CO_2 emissions (*www.gestalten.com/myclimate*).